Paul Engelbert

A Locomotives International Publication

Above:	*A steam-headed freight train on the Szilvásvarad Forestry Railway. Photo courtesy of the Közlekedési Múzeum.*
Front Cover:	*Mk48,404 (formerly Mk,2037) at Szalajka-fátolyveses. The class Mk48 diesels on the Szilvásvárad system retained their MÁV livery. Photo: Paul Engelbert, 22nd June 1994.*
Rear Cover:	*C50 number 2 of the Csömöder Forestry Railway has almost reached Oltárc. Photo: Paul Engelbert, 10th July 1996.*
Title Page:	*The first of the class Mk48 owned by the state forestry railways, in a narrow curve near Andokút in July 1996. The loco was built by Rába (033/1961) for the Lillafüred line, where it remains, now numbered D02-508. Photo: Paul Engelbert.*

ISBN 1-900340-09-7
First Edition. Published by Paul Catchpole Ltd., 47 Glenwood Road, Kings Norton, Birmingham, B38 8HE, England
Edited and typeset by Paul Catchpole, printed and bound by Spectrum Digital Imaging, Leamore Lane, Walsall.

Forestry Railways in Hungary

Paul Engelbert

Contents

Preface

Today Hungarian railway enthusiasts are very well organised. Much fragmented historical material which has survived the communist period has now been collected and published in books and even on the internet. Unfortunately the subject of forestry railways is not very well documented. Above all the literature which is available about Hungarian forestry railways is written in the Hungarian language only, which makes it virtually inaccesible for foreigners.

Because I was anxious to know more about this subject I started to learn some Hungarian words, which made it possible for me to understand the basic information in a Hungarian text. In my letters to the forestry railway companies I requested additional information and of course I also acquired information during my visits to Hungary.

Surprisingly, a relatively large amount of information about the communist period has survived in primary sources. Unfortunately much pre-war material seems to be lost and this lack of information especially concerns the rolling stock, and information about the communist period is still full of gaps. Because after the Second World War an enormous number of narrow gauge railways were built, rolling stock was often exchanged between serveral railways, making it hard to trace the individual locomotives and wagons. Also, little is known about short or temporary railways which were often built in inaccesible areas. It was not always possible to trace all locomotives and their numbers or corresponding dates, because even the best information, provided by the Hungarian narrow gauge society (KBK), is still not fully accurate.

Undoubtetly the well-informed reader will find details which are incorrect or missing, therefore I would like to emphasise that I do not pretend this publication will give a complete and definitive view of the Hungarian forestry railways, however, I do hope that it will contribute to the knowledge about this interesting subject. Any corrections and additional material will be welcome.

Finally I would like to thank all the people who have supplied information and photographs and have corrected the text and the locomotive lists. My special thanks go out to the following people (in alphabetical order):

- Imre Balogh, Zamárdi
- Roland Beier, Wien
- Gábor Chikán, Budapest
- Helge Ralf Harling, Nienburg
- Hans Hufnagel, Ebreichsdorf
- Jörg Körner, Graz
- Steven van Luyn, Nijmegen
- Marco Moerland, Schiedam
- Quirinus Reichen, Frutigen
- György Villányi, Budapest

Paul Engelbert, Alphen aan den Rijn, January 1999

Introduction

Hungarian forestry railways are not well known in Western Europe despite the fact that since the late 1960s there have been few obstacles to visiting and photographing these railways. Because they were rapidly modernised in the 1950s and 1960s they were probably not so interesting for those railway enthusiasts who are mainly steam orientated. Ironically because of modernisation, nowadays a large number of forestry railways still exist. In fact, Hungary is the country with relatively the most forestry railways in Europe, and indeed in the world.

Many but not all forestry railways have lost their timber traffic and are reduced to tourist attractions, but the scenery, the layout of the track, the depots, the stations, the rolling stock and the ever present sawmill still reveal the original purpose of these lines. Whereas almost all the more famous forestry railways in the neighbouring and much poorer Romainia have been closed in past years, the remaining Hungarian lines generally seem to flourish.

In this publication the histories of all present day forestry railways in Hungary are reviewed, with the emphasis on the description of the development of each line and its social and economic importance then and now. Only locomotives which are known to have run on the present forestry railways are listed. For the most common and most special types some technical details are given.

In the following pages, first the development of forestry railways in Hungary is described then we take a more detailed look at the present motive power; the class C50 and class Mk48 diesels. The following chapters deal with the individual forestry railways which are still operational, describing for each network the most important historical facts and the present situation. A detailed map of each network shows the lines still in existence and those already closed. For each locomotive of the individual railways the number, the manufacturer, the class (between brackets the works type) and the period of service are listed. An overview of all known forestry railways in Hungary completes the publication.

Number 2 of the Lenti Forestry Railway with a freight train at Sárdipuszta.
Photo: Jörg Körner.

The History of Forestry Railways in Hungary

Railway history is always closely linked to economic history. The northern and south-western parts of Hungary are covered with forests which provide an almost inexhaustible source of timber. In the second half of the 19th century the large scale extraction of the timber supplies began in Hungary and indeed in the whole of central Europe.

Private companies acquired the necessary concessions and erected steam or water-driven sawmills. From nearby forests the logs were initially transported to the sawmill by oxen or horses. Rain made the transportation of logs very difficult, especially in Autumn, sometimes even interrupting the sawmill's timber supply for several days.

Trees which were felled further away were floated down rivers to the sawmill. Floating was very hazardous for the raftmen, who could fall into the river and drown or get jammed between the heavy trees. Floating was of course only possible in valleys with a relatively long and wide river. An alternative method of transporting logs was a log chute or flume, which could be seen in valleys with only a narrow and shallow natural water-course. By transporting the logs through a chute or by floating them the quality of the timber deteriorated because of the constant contact with the water. This problem would not occur if railways were used to transport the logs out of the woods to the sawmill, indeed railways have been used for this purpose since the 1870s. Such railways made it possible to cut extended forestry areas in a profitable way. The timber transport was safe for the workmen and relatively independent of weather conditions.

Forestry railways mainly ran from the forests to the sawmill but some also connected the sawmill to the local railway station or even to a harbour. The permanent main lines opened up the larger valleys. Sometimes temporary lines were built to connect loading points in side valleys to the main line. Most forestry railway systems reached a length of approximately 10 km, but there were only a handfull of networks of more than 40 km, the largest being the 76 km long Csömödér system.

Most forestry railways only ran uphill from the sawmill to the loading points in the forests. In such cases only light trains with empty wagons had to be pulled uphill and the heavy loaded trains took advantage of gravity on their way down the valley to the sawmill. When the line had a constant steep gradient the loaded wagons could even run on their own downhill to the sawmill, relying solely on gravity. This gravitation propulsion was used on most forestry railways in mountain areas, like for instance the Felsőtárkány, the Kemence and the Pálháza systems.

In order to minimize costs the track had to follow the meandering river valleys without tunnels, viaducts and intensive ground works and the rolling stock had to be very simple and easy to maintain, therefore the forestry railways are exclusively narrow gauge. The most common gauges are 600 mm and 760 mm, which makes it possible to use curves as sharp as 30 metres.

Steep gradients had to be overcome by laying the track in large loops. If the valley was too narrow the trains sometimes had to run alternately backwards and forewards, zig-zagging up the slopes. In Hungary this procedure was carried out on the Nagybörszöny network. If the gradient became too steep for an adhesion railway an inclined plane was erected. Near Szilvásvárad and between Csömödér and Vétyem such an inclined plane was integrated into a railway system. A point of note is that forestry railways never used a rack rail.

The use of forestry railways in Hungary began relatively late in comparison to the surrounding areas which had also been under Hungarian control until 1920. Already by the turn of the century forestry railways were used on a large scale in present day

After the Second World War many new lines were built, but also many short horse worked lines were closed. In 1948 a group of officials visited the line from Simongát to Pollai erdő, which was closed in the same year.

Photo: collection of Imre Balogh.

Until the introduction of the class C50 diesel engines in the 1950s, small steam locomotives were the standard motive power on Hungarian forestry railways. This 0-6-0T seen at Paphegy on 10th September 1957 was built by Orenstein & Koppel (8435/1917).

Photo: László Mohay.

Slovakia, Romania and the Ukraine. At that time only a handful of lines existed in today's Hungary but many others were planned. Some of these were realised before the First World War broke out in 1914. They were relatively short and therefore almost exclusively used horses to pull the wagons. The heyday of Hungarian forestry railways began in the early 1920s as many railway systems, which were presumably already planned before the war, opened to traffic and existing networks were extended.

Not all forestry railways were used exclusively for the transportation of timber. Some lines also connected a coal mine or quarry with the standard gauge railway station. Such semi-industrial forestry railways were mainly found in the mountainous areas in the north of the country. On the main lines of the Gyöngyös, Debrecen and Lillafüred forestry railways a public passenger service was operated.

More and more forestry railways were using steam engines instead of horses. The Budapest works and Orenstein & Koppel built most of the locos and some forestry railways acquired abandoned steam engines of the kkHB and the DHF which had been built in Austria and Germany during the war. In 1929 the Lillafüred forestry railway even introduced modern petrol-driven railcars and two years later the Debrecen forestry railway followed their example. Despite the success of these vehicles the motorisation of the forestry railways did not carry on. In the 1920s and 1930s petrol driven locomotives were not yet very reliable and above all, the steam engines which had been bought by the time the lines were opened were still only a few years old.

After the Second World War Hungary fell under a communist regime and soon the process of forced nationalisation of private agricultural, industrial and railway companies began. In 1945 the private forestry estates and their railway systems were nationalised and administered by the state forestry company MÁLLERD. The ownership of the other forestry railways which were not part of a private forestry estate did not change until 1949 when private industrial companies and private railway companies were nationalised.

Since 1949 almost all forestry railways have been operated by the state forestry railway company Állami Erdei Vasutak (ÁEV). The ÁEV held an office in Budapest and although officially the ÁEV lines were run from this Budapest office, the individual forestry railways remained for the greater part independent. The ÁEV was mainly a strategic organisation which for example co-ordinated the exchange of rolling stock between the lines and introduced a uniform numbering scheme.

After the ÁEV had taken over the forestry railways some networks were extended. Even some complete new systems like for instance the one at Gemenc were built. Also the ÁEV increased the number of forestry railways which operated a public passenger service to a total of sixteen and all forestry railways which operated such a service were published in the special ÁEV section of the official Hungarian timetable.

Most important, the ÁEV modernised the rolling stock. In the 1950s the introduction of diesel motive power began, making almost all steam locos redundant, but some steamers still survived until the 1970s on the forestry railways of Csömödér, Királyrét and Lillafüred. The class C50 diesel engine became the standard motive power for almost all narrow gauge railways in Hungary, thus also for the ÁEV.

Some forestry railways were not taken over by the ÁEV in 1949. Instead they were administered by the National Economy Railway Company (Gazdasági Vasutak Nemzeti Vallalat). This organisation operated a large number of narrow gauge agricultural and industrial railways throughout the whole country. In 1955 the GVI took over all lines and operated them until 1960. Most former GVI lines have been run by the MÁV GV since, but the forestry railways of Lenti and Galgamácsa were taken over by the ÁEV.

Because of low oil prices and the mass introducation of motorised transport the forestry railways began to lose freight to road traffic

In 1989 the Kaszó Forestry Railway still ran freight trains. On 3rd April 1989 C401 was photographed shunting at Bojsa kitérő.

Photo: Jörg Körner.

in the 1960s. Lorries and tractors could use the recently built forest roads, so some smaller networks were subsequently closed. Most line closures were the result of the traffic and transport concept of 1968, which was aimed at a more efficient transport system. Inefficient narrow gauge lines were closed and the traffic diverted to the roads. The new concept meant the end for most Hungarian narrow gauge industrial, agricultural and local railways, but remarkably not for the forestry railways, however, this does not mean that the ÁEV closed no lines at all.

In 1970 the ÁEV still operated 24 lines, including 15 lines with passenger traffic. Ten years later the number of ÁEV lines was reduced to approximately 16. Twelve of them still operated a passenger service. The Kemence, Lenti and Vitézipuszta networks were freight only. In 1990 only 14 ÁEV lines existed. The same 12 lines of 1980 operated a passenger service but freight trains only ran in Lenti, Csömöder, Mesztegnyő, Gemenc, Kemence, Gyöngyös, Almamellék and Lillafüred. By that time all other networks had already lost the transport of timber and other freight and have only operated a passenger service since. The remaining ÁEV lines only use diesel engines, but some of the old steam engines have been retained as a monument at the local sawmill or at the railway museum in Nagycenk.

After the iron curtain had fallen in 1989 Hungary became a democratic republic which quickly westernised. Even though forestry railways are seen as relics of the past in Western Europe, all but two of the Hungarian forestry railways have remained in service. The Nagybörzsöny network was closed in 1991. The Kemence system followed in 1992. Since 1992 new private forestry companies and regional communities have operated the forestry railways, however, the infrastructure has remained state property.

Present day motive power and the increasingly common function of forestry railways as tourist and leisure facilities are both represented in this view of Mk48-404 at Szalajka-Fatelep on 22nd June 1994.

Photo: Paul Engelbert.

Motive Power

Today the forestry railways only use three types of diesel engine and on every railway one or more class C50 is present. Some lines in the north also use the heavier four axle class Mk48. Only in Szilvásvárad is a class Ns3 (or L60) still to be found. The history and the technical details of the C50 and Mk48 are reviewed below. The class Ns3 is described in the chapter about the Szilvásvárad Forestry Railway.

Class C50

In order to understand the history of the class C50 diesel engines we have to go back to the Second World War. In 1944 the retreating German army caused much damage to Hungarian railway lines, including many narrow gauge industrial and agricultural railways (gazdasági vasutak; GV). By the end of the Second World War almost all these lines were either damaged or completely destroyed.

Three years after the war had ended the reconstuction of approximately 2500 kilometers of narrow gauge GV lines began. This was co-ordinated by the Gazdasági Vasutak Igazgatósága (GVI), an organisation which was formed by both the departments of traffic and agriculture on 1st August 1947. Under the leading role of the GVI the damaged GV networks were reconstucted and in many cases extended. Above all many new GV networks were built. Most heavier GV lines had a gauge of 760 mm.

The GVI needed many new diesel locomotives to replace the prewar steam engines. More new motive power was needed for the new networks and the extensions of existing networks. Therefore MÁV Északi főműhely in Budapest (Északi fm) developed a small two-axle diesel locomotive. This class C50 locomotive was equipped with a 50 HP Csepel-Steyr D413 diesel engine and mechanical transmission, which was also used in Csepel trucks. Their maximum speed was 30 km/h.

Between 1953 and 1966 Északi fm built a total of approximately 210 class C50 for railways in Hungary and another 20 class C50 were exported to North-Korea. In the early 1970s the MÁV narrow gauge workshop in Dombovár (Kisvasutak Műhelye Dombovár; KMD) constructed some additional class C50.

The class C50 diesel engines were delivered in a sub-type with an inside frame (GVI class 3700) and a sub-type with an outside frame (GVI class 5700). Északi fm built a total of 93 class 3700 and 38 class 5700 for the GVI. Other sub-types are relatively rare, such as the special 600/950/1000 mm gauge variant with its somewhat pointed nose. There is also a shorter and lighter sub-type of the class C50. These engines were numbered 4501 - 4512. The second position of the number indicates that they have a weight of only 5000 kg, whereas the normal C50 have a weight of 7000 kg.

Északi fm also delivered class C50 to other industrial railways, to the MÁV and to the ÁEV. On the forestry railways of the ÁEV, which were technically mainly identical to GV lines, the C50 were very successful. Only some 35 class C50 were delivered directly to the ÁEV but as more and more GV-lines were closed in the 1960s and 1970s the ÁEV bought many redundant class C50 off the MÁV GV (the former GVI). The ÁEV posesses all known sub-types but the former GVI class 3700 is the most common.

Almost all forestry railways have used one or more class C50. Nowadays the class C50 diesel locomotive is still the standard motive power for the forestry railways, except for the lines of Királyrét, Gyöngyos, Szilvásvárad and Lillafüred, where they have been replaced by the heavier class Mk48 diesels.

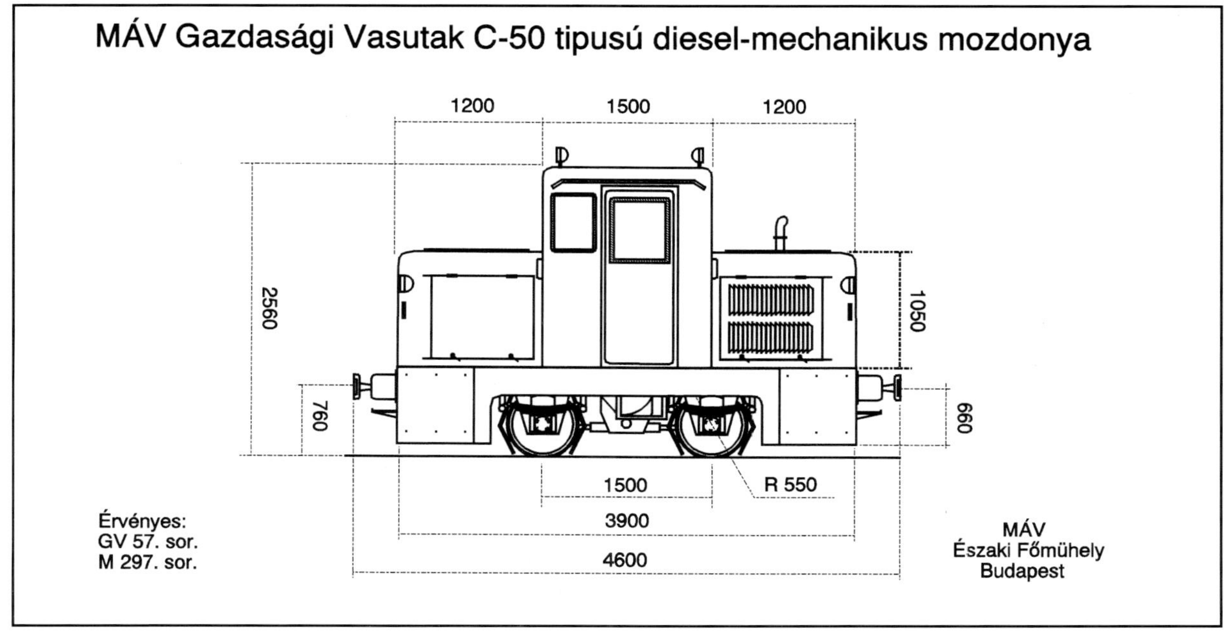

C402 of the ÁEV Kaszó line represents the GVI class 3700. Through the open door the throttle pedal (right) and brake pedal (left) can clearly be distinguished.
Photo: Paul Engelbert.

Class Mk48

The class C50 diesel locomotives were actually too light for the narrow gauge local lines of the MÁV. Therefore in 1958 the Rába machine factory in Győr (formerly Wilhelm Pieck Wagon és-Gépgyár) developed two prototypes of a heavy four-axle diesel locomotive. These narrow gauge locomotives (works type M040) were based on the MÁV standard gauge class M28,1 shunting engines. With its 96 kW engine the M040 was almost three times more powerful than a class C50, although the maximum speed was still only 30 km/h.

Apparently the prototypes were succesful because in 1959 Rába delivered a further ten M040. The MÁV numbered these Mk48,1001 - Mk48,1010. The M stands for motor locomotive, k for narrow gauge (keskenynyomközű vasút) and the 4 indicates that it is a four-axle locomotive. Later both prototypes, which were initially numbered M492,001 and 002, were renumbered Mk48,1011 and Mk48,1012. The class Mk48,1 were stationed on the MÁV local railways of Szeged, Kecskemét, Nyíregyháza, Békéscsaba and Sárospatak and on the Oroszlány industrial railway, which was operated by the MÁV GV.

In 1960 Rába delivered ten somewhat modernised M040 to the MÁV. This is the works type M041. The M041 was given a hydraulic driving unit and a 100 kW Ganz-Jendrassik 6 Js diesel engine. The M041 had a maximum speed of 30 km/h while shunting and 50 km/h while hauling a train on the main line. Externally

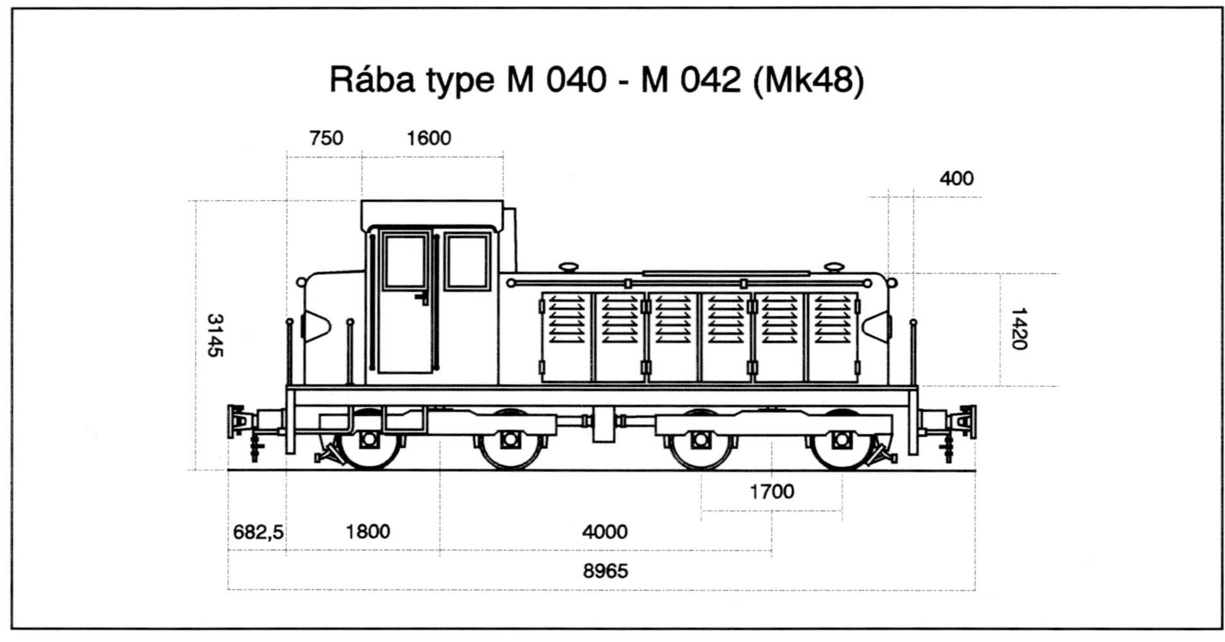

Mk48,409 at Lajosháza on 29th June 1997. Engine drivers and conductors on the Mátravasút system are teenagers as this was formerly a 'pioneer' railway.
Photo: Paul Engelbert.

the M041 was identical to the M040. The MÁV numbered these engines Mk48,2001 - Mk48,2010 and stationed them on all MÁV narrow gauge lines plus the industrial railway of Oroszlány.

The class Mk48,2 diesel locomotives were more succesful than their diesel mechanical sisters. In 1961 Rába even exported ten engines of the export type M042 to Czechoslovakian forestry railways and after these M042 had been delivered Rába built an M041 for the Lillafüred forestry railway. For many years this engine has been the only Mk48 of the ÁEV. Finally the MÁV ordered a further 29 M041, which were delivered in the second half of 1961, and numbered these engines Mk48,2011 - Mk48,2039.

In the 1960s and 1970s the MÁV and MÁV GV closed many of their narow gauge lines, therefore many locomotives were withdrawn. In the early 1970s the class Mk48,1 was already superflous. Three of them went to the Lillafüred forestry railway, where they were in service until the 1980s.

After the MÁV had also closed the Szeged local railway (1976) and the Bodrogközi local railway (1980) the ÁEV was even able to obtain fourteen modern class Mk48,2. The ÁEV stationed them on just four of its northern Hungarian networks (Lillafüred, Szilvásvárad, Gyöngyös and Királyrét). They are all still in active service.

The 1966 ÁEV numbering scheme

In 1966 the ÁEV introduced a numbering scheme for all their lines. Each network or group of neighbouring networks received a unique number, which was used to identify the rolling stock belonging to that specific line or lines. The number also gave information about the type of vehicle and the axle-weight. The numbers have the positions **Xaa-bcc**. Their meaning is explained below.

X	**vehicle type**
C	C50
D	Mk48, Ns3
E	MD40

aa	**forestry railway network**
01	Pálháza
02	Lillfüred
03	Felsőtárkány
04	Szilvásvárad
05	Gyöngyös
06	Királyrét
07	Nagybörzsöny
08	Kemence, Bernecebarati, Diósjenő
09	Süttő
10	Császár
11	Réde
12	Franciavágás
13	Devecser
14	Lenti
15	Csömödér
16	Mesztengnyő
17	Kaszó
18	Simongát
19	Dalmand
20	?
21	Almamellék
22	Vitézipuszta
23	Csányoszró
24	Gemenc

b **axle weight (in tons)**

cc **unique identification number**

Examples:

C16-402 was a class C50, stationed on the Mesztegnyő system, with an axle-weight of 4 tons and running number 2.

D02-508 was a class Mk48, stationed on the Lillafüred system, with an axle-weight of 5 tons and running number 8.

The 1995 ÁEV numbering scheme

In 1995 the 1966 numbering scheme was slightly altered. The numbers have the following positions:
ÁEV **aa X-bcc**.

aa	**forestry railway network**
01	Pálháza
02	Lillfüred
03	Szilvásvárad
04	Felsőtárkány
05	Gyöngyös
06	Királyrét
07	Nagybörzsöny
08	Gemenc
09	Almamellék
10	Mesztengnyő
11	Kaszó
12	Csömödér
13	Lenti

X	**vehicle type (C50, Mk48; not shortened)**
b	**axle weight (in tons)**
cc	**unique identification number**

Examples:

ÁEV 03 C50-406 is a class C50 of the Felsőtárkány system with an axle-weight of 4 tons and engine number 6.

ÁEV 05 Mk48-404 is a class Mk48 of the Gyöngyos system with an axle-weight of 4 tons and engine number 4.

On 27th May 1973 the diesel mechanical D02-503 (ex-MÁV Mk48,1003) had only been in service on the Lillafüred Forestry Railway for 13 days. The locomotive was photographed in Miskolc. Photo: Jan Havelaar, courtesy of Marco Moerland.

The Current Situation

Nowadays only the forestry railways at Lenti, Csömödér and Gemenc are regulary used for the transportation of timber. It is expected that these lines will manage to keep freight trains running in the future, but it may be that freight traffic will be resumed on other forestry railways soon. The first occasional freight trains have already been observed in Kaszó and Almamellék. However, for most forestry railways passenger trains will remain the most important source of income. Because of an improving economic situation a growing number of Hungarians can afford a weekend trip or short holiday. Luckily many forestry railways are situated in the important tourist regions in the north of the country, and they already benefit from the growing number of Hungarian and foreign tourists. On the forestry railway of Kaszó it is possible to travel by steam train, making this railway even more interesting for both tourists and railway enthusiasts. Shortly, steam trains will also run at Csömöder, Szilvásvárad, and maybe Lillafüred.

Whereas the future of the forestry railways of Pálháza, Lillafüred, Szilvásvárad, Felsőtárkány, Gyönyös and Királyrét seems to be secured, the fate of the passenger-only lines in the south of the country is very unclear. The official timetables for the passenger service on the lines at Mesztegnyő, Almamellék and Kaszó are unreliable. Until recently most of the time the trains did not run at all, however this situation seems to be changing. A large number of the trains which are published in the official timetable are actually running again.

Ten years after the iron curtain was drawn aside the forestry railway companies seem to have recovered from the economic crisis. Everywhere the neglected track and rolling stock is being repaired. Also there are many plans for new branch lines. The most important one is the connection between the Csömödér and the Lenti system, which is due to be opened to traffic in 1999.

The forestry railways find themselves gaining more and more public interest. Since 1994 a society of railway enthusiasts has collected the rolling stock of narrow gauge local, industrial, agricultural and forestry railways at the open air museum in Kecskemét. Also since 1994 annual narrow gauge railway days have been organised on all of the forestry railways. On these days a festival is organised at the main station and often there are special trains for railway enthusiasts. More importantly, in 1997 a group of railway enthusiasts started to repair the track and rolling stock of the former Szob-Nagybörzsöny Forestry Railway. The future timetable was published in the 1998 MÁV timetable.

Loading timber at Szilvágy on the Lenti Forestry Railway.
Photo: Helge Ralf Harling.

The Pálháza Forestry Railway

The oldest forestry railway in present day Hungary was built in the Zemplén mountains in the north-eastern part of the country. In 1888 a seven kilometre long 700 mm gauge railway was opened on Count Karoly's forestry estate. The line ran from the Count's hunting-lodge on a small hill in Kőkapő through the Kemencepatak valley to the sawmill near Pálháza. The transportation of timber was the only purpose of the railway. In 1903 the forestry railway was extended by 4 km to Susulya, for which it was necessary to dig a tunnel through the hill at Kőkapő. Later other lines were built in some side valleys and the network reached a total length of 14 km.

In 1924 the Hegykőzi Vasút (HV) opened a typical Hungarian 760 mm gauge local economy railway which ran from Sátoraljaújhely to Pálháza and further on to Fűzérkomlós. At the terminus of the forestry railway near Pálháza, the HV erected the Pálháza-ipartelep station, but because through traffic between the forestry railway and the HV line was not possible due to the different gauges, the timber had to be transhipped at Pálháza-ipartelep. Nevertheless the HV line was an important improvement of the transport system in this region. The timber trade increased drastically and as a result of this so did traffic on the 700 mm gauge forestry railway.

After the private estate of Count Károlyi had been nationalised in 1947 the forestry railway was regauged to 760 mm so that wagons could be exchanged with the Hegykőzi Vasút. Again timber traffic on the Pálháza forestry railway intensified.

The revival of the freight traffic on the railway did not last long though due to mass motorisation and the building of forest roads in the Zemplén mountain area. Because the timber could be transported not only from the forests to the sawmill at Pálháza, but also further on the Hegykőzi Vasút to Sátoraljaújhely and Sárospatak, the relatively short forestry railway managed to remain open to freight traffic.

After the MÁV had closed the Hegykőzi Vasút on 29 November 1980, the through working of timber wagons was no longer possible. The state forestry organisation decided that freight trains should not run exclusively for the transportation of timber on the relatively short distance from the forests to the Pálháza sawmill and diverted the timber traffic completely to the road.

In 1958 the ÁEV opened a passenger service on the 7 km long section between Pálháza-ipartlep and Kőkapű. The trains were not used by regular passengers because the railway did not connect villages of any importance, however, the forests on the Zemplén mountains attracted many tourists and nature lovers so the railway was ensured of sufficient patronage. After freight traffic on the forestry railway had ended in 1980 the passenger service was, as it was called, 'temporary paused'. Afterwards the track and rolling stock remained in place but were no longer maintained.

Almost nine years later the origional seven kilometre long section between Pálháza-ipartelep and Kőkapű was renewed and opened again to passenger traffic on 15th August 1989. The next year the passenger service was extended to Rostalló, on the other side of the tunnel at Kőkapű.

Trains only run during the tourist season from the beginning of May until half way through October, offering work to six employees, but the former forestry railway has turned out to be a great success. In 1995 30,214 passengers travelled between Pálháza-ipartelep and Rostalló but because the railway began about 1 km south-west of the village of Pálháza the number of tourists using the train still remained below expectation, therefore in 1996 the line was extended from Pálháza-ipartelep to Pálháza village. The new 1.3 km long railway section used exactly the same route as the

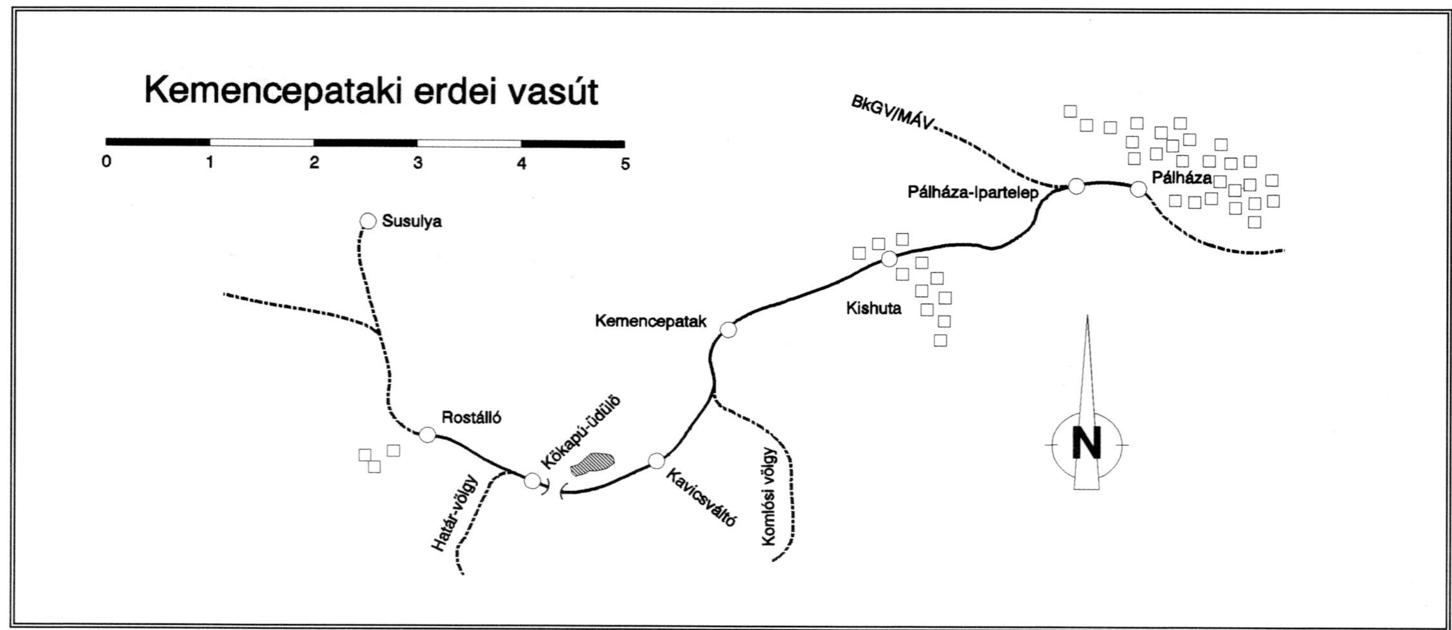

C01-402 stands on the line leading to the single-track engine shed at Pálháza ipartelep, which is still in use. Photo: Jörg Körner.

former HV economy railway, even ending at the former HV station at Pálháza. The official opening of this section took place on 17th August 1996 and the following year no less than 37,000 passengers travelled, and the number is still rising.

Rolling Stock

During the first years of traffic the trains were hauled by horses and only after fourteen years, in 1902, did the first steam engine appear on the line. Unfortunately nothing is known about this loco except that it caused many forest fires and for this reason it was withdrawn from the line in 1906, after which again only horses were used. In 1924 due to intensified freight traffic steam traction was reintroduced in the form of a small Krauss locomotive.

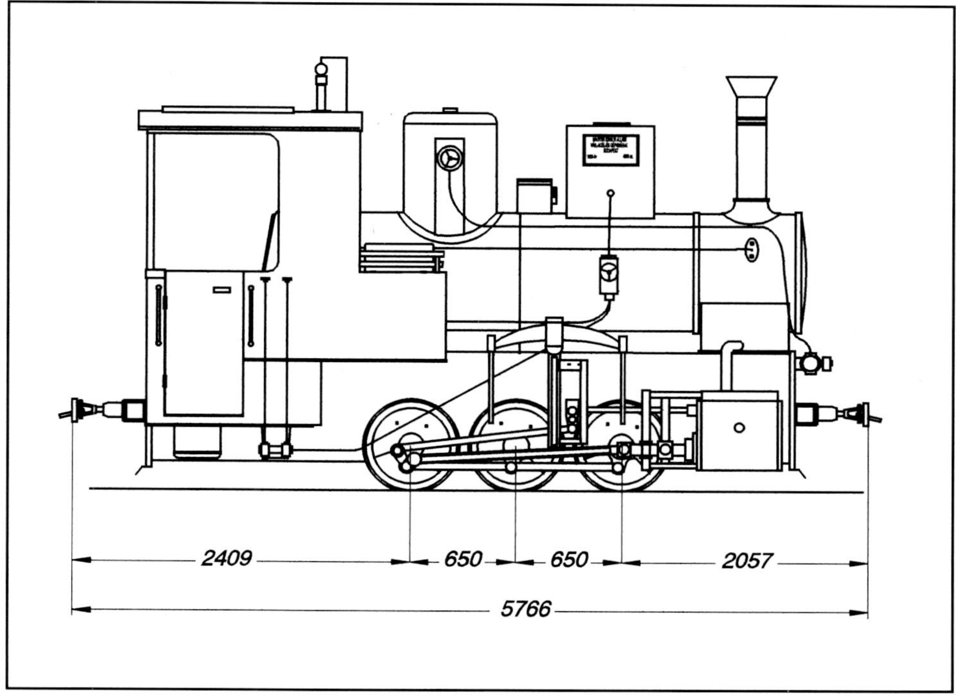

The Budapest class 106

After the Second World War the railway received three second hand 0-6-0T,

MÁVAG type 106. One of these engines was the former Kecskemét economy railway (KGV) number III which in the 1930s the KGV had converted into an 0-6-2T with enlarged water tanks. In 1940 the MÁV hired the loco and numbered it 394,205. This unusual class 394 was mainly used on the Cegléd - Tiszajenő economy railway (CGV). In 1963 the loco came to Pálháza.

In 1964 two modern class C50 diesel engines with inside frames representing the MÁV GV class 3700 arrived at Pálháza, replacing the older steam engines and nowadays the railway is worked with class C50 engines only.

Company	Name
1888 - 1947:	Count Karolyi forestry estate
1947 - 1949:	MÁLLERD
1949 - 1991:	ÁEV
1991:	Északerdő Rt

Name of the line	
1888 - 1949:	Kemencepataki erdei vasút
1949 - 1992:	Pálházai Állami Erdei Vasút
1992:	Kemencepataki erdei vasút

Locomotives of the Pálháza Forestry Railway

Number(s)	Manufacturer	Class	In Service	Remarks
357,311 *Bimbo*	KrMü (7301/1920)	0-6-0T (27cs)	1924-1961	ex-Újlak *Ubu*
357,313	Bp (4877/1925)	0-6-0T (106)	1954-?	ex-Haricavölgyi iparvasút 7
"Bimbo"	Bp (4878/1925)	0-6-0T (106)	1954-?	ex-Haricavölgyi iparvasút 8; preserved at Pálháza
394,205	Bp (4865/1928)	0-6-2T (106)	1963-1970s	ex-MÁV 394,205; ex-KGV III
DEV-1; C01-401	Éfm (../1954)	C50	1964-now	
C01-402	Éfm (../1953)	C50	1964-now	
C01-403	Éfm (../1955)	C50	1994-now	ex-FÁEV C03-402

C01-402 with a passenger train to Pálháza on 31st August 1991. On this hot day the open summer coach was very popular. Photo: Jörg Körner.

The Lillafüred Forestry Railway

The Bükk mountain area is situated in the north of the country, between Miskolc and Eger. The peaks are up to 950 metres above sea level and covered with beech forest, which gives the area its name (bükk is Hungarian for beech). In 1976 a large part of the Bükk mountain area was declared a national park.

On 4th October 1920 a 760 mm gauge forestry railway was opened in the east of the Bükk mountains with a 17.7 kilometre long main line starting at the Saint Anna Church in Miskolc and running via Lillafüred to Garadna. A number of branch lines were opened in 1921 and 1922. The most important, which was in effect another main line, branched off at Papírgyár (paper factory). Originally it ended after 11 kilometers at Mahóca, but in 1940 was extended to Taksalápa and in 1947 to Faskasgödör-Örvénykő (km 18.8).

The other branch lines were much shorter. A line of just 2 km from Lillafüred was built to the loading point at Kerekhegy. The timber storage depot at Ládi, where the timber could be loaded onto standard gauge wagons, was connected to the forestry railway by a 2.9 km branch which started near the station of Diósgyőr. From Ládi another 4.5 km line ran to the loading point at Vásárhely. The network reached a total length of 45 km, with approximately one third situated in the built-up areas of Miskolc and Diósgyőr.

Both at Pereces kitérő (Pereces crossing) and Ságvári an industrial railway, the 1000 mm gauge Perecesi kisvasút (Pereces - Diósgyőr Vasgyár), crossed the forestry railway and connected mines north of Diósgyőr to the Diósgyőr iron works. The forestry railway depot was situated further west near Majláth station. Here there are numerous tracks, an engine shed, a workshop and the railway's staff office. In this westerly direction the railway lies on forest-covered hills which surround the Szinva valley and 13 kilometres beyond Pereces crossing is Lillafüred, where the small station is situated right between the only two tunnels on the line. From Lillafüred to the terminus at Garadna the line runs through the Garadna valley.

The layout of the line from Papírgyár to Farkasgödor is completely different and this is probably the most spectacular section of all Hungarian forestry railways. Constructed with steep gradients and curves as sharp as 40 metres, the line traverses an uninhabited mountain area north of Lillafüred.

The railway's main task was the transport of timber from the forests to Ládi fatelep, however, the trains also carried coal from the Márta mine to the iron works and paper factory in Diósgyőr. An extensive operation to transport dolomite for the iron works in Ózd began in 1950s. The ÁEV carried the dolomite to Ládi fatelep and the MÁV was responsible for transportation through to Ózd.

Above all on 3rd May 1924 a passenger service between Miskolc and Garadna was started. Most passengers were tourists who

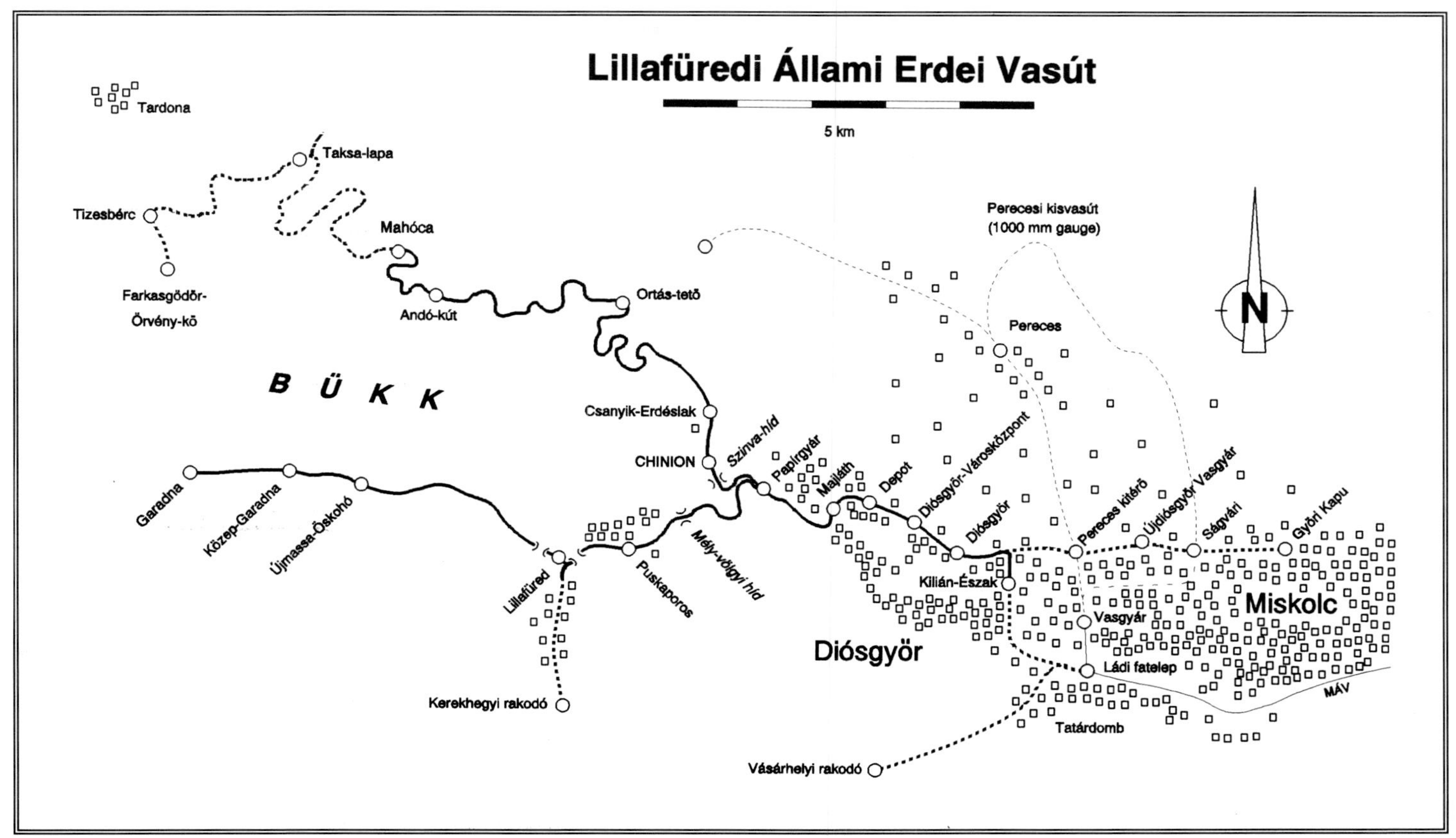

The LÁEV was one of the few Hungarian forestry railways to use a large number of heavy 0-8-0Ts, in this case five Budapest type 85 and four Budapest type 70 engines. In 1957 one of the type 70s (467,602) was photographed at Majláth.
Photo: László Mohay.

The Lillafüred Forestry Railway is famous for its diesel railcars. Jan Havelaar photographed A02-601 with two trailers in Miskolc on 27th May 1973.
Collection of Marco Moerland.

stayed at the Palota hotel in Lillafüred, built between 1927 and 1929. Since 1963 passenger trains have also run on the Farkasgödör branch line and during the 1960s about 300,000 passengers travelled on the railway every year.

In the 1970s the forestry railway began to lose freight to road haulage and in 1982 all freight except timber was diverted to the roads. The remaining timber transport ended around 1991 and afterwards the freight only lines to Kerekhegy and Ládi were closed. (Traffic on the Ládi - Vásárhely branch line had already ceased in 1934). Not only branch lines but also a few kilometres of the main line were closed, and since September 1979 trains have no longer run through the residential quarters on the west side of Miskolc, now closely built up. The new terminus of Kilián-Észak, which is meanwhile also surrounded by high appartment buildings, is situated just north of the Dorottya utca, the main road between Miskolc and Diósgyőr.

Nowadays the railway is operated solely for the benefit of tourists, and in fact between Miskolc and Garadna the trains run all year round, although in Summer the frequency is higher than in Winter. The line is well patronised, for example in 1997 the Lillafüred Forestry Railway carried 192,000 passengers.

The Papírgyár - Farkasgödör branch line is now only used for special trains, although the timetable shows three trains a day at weekends. Even these trains have run no further than Mahóca since the early 1990s because the track on the Mahóca - Farkasgödör section is in a very poor condition. The Papírgyár - Mahóca section was renewed in 1996 and there are serious plans to reconstruct the Mahóca - Taksalápa section as well. The remaining Taksalápa - Farkasgödör section will probably be abandoned, but instead it may be that a new line will be built from Taksalápa to the town of Tardona, some four kilometers north-west of Farkasgödör.

Rolling Stock

The Lillafüred forestry railway was steam worked from the beginning. With the exception of two O&K engines the railway only used Budapest-built locomotives, some of which were purchased new, though most were bought second hand.

A number of these engines have an interesting history. LÁEV 2 and 3, for instance, were originally built for the Slovakian FGV (nowadays the ČHŽ - Čierny Balog - Hronec), where they would have been numbered III and IV, but because Slovakia was separated from Hungary after the First World War the locomotives were not delivered to the FGV. Instead FGV III was supplied to the LÁEV and FGV IV went to a Hungarian mine railway. After a few years this engine also came to Lillafüred.

Steam engine number 1 was originally built for a forestry railway in Transylvania. Like FGV III and IV this loco probably never ran there and also came straight to Lillafüred. During the Second World War LÁEV 1 was temporarily used by the MÁV, where she was numbered 492,105 and from 1941 until approximately 1942 she ran on the strategic railway from Marosvásárhely (Târgu Mureș) to Szászlekence (Lechința) in Transylvania.

447,401 was a very special engine, an 0-8-0 of Budapest type 135, one of the six engines of this type delivered to Hungarian railways in 1954. The other 234 type 135 were sent as reparations to the Soviet Union, where they ran as class Kv-4. Number 447,401 is the largest steam engine that ever ran on a forestry railway in Hungary. After diesel traction had made this locomotive redundant it was preserved at Majláth. Remarkably, in 1996 447,401 was sent to the workshop of the museum forestry railway at Čierny Balog in Slovakia, where it was to be restored to working order again, but unfortunately the engine returned to Miskolc in 1998, still not operational. The railway hopes that a steam engine will in due course attract more tourists than the diesel engines which normally haul passenger trains on the the Lillafüred system.

In 1929 Ganz delivered two railcars which were used for the passenger service between Miskolc and Garadna. These four-axle petrol driven units were modern for the time and very luxurious, as much so as the four-axle coaches that were used as reinforcements in the busy summer period. In 1940 both railcars were equipped with new and more powerful diesel engines, which improved their performance on steep gradients. They ran on the Budapest pioneer railway in the 1950s and returned to Miskolc after the new class Mk49 had been stationed in Budapest. A02-601 was withdrawn in 1980 but A02-602 remained in service until 1992. Afterwards she went to the Budapest pioneer railway for a second time, where she was completely restored. Since 1996 this beautiful railcar has again run in the Budapest hills.

In the 1950s the steam engines were replaced by diesels. Between 1954 and 1963 seven small class C50 came to Miskolc. In the 1970s they were in their turn replaced by second-hand class Mk48. A few diesel mechanical engines (Rába type M040) also ran in the Bükk mountains but they were soon replaced by their more powerful diesel hydraulic sisters of type M041. Two M040 belonging to the MÁV had run trials on the Lillafüred Rorestry Railway in 1959, and apparently these were successful because in 1961 Rába delivered an M041 directly to the ÁEV at Miskolc. This engine, numbered M8, was the only class Mk48 on the ÁEV for many years. Nowdays all trains are hauled by one of four M041. The only remaining C50 is probably not in working order any more.

Name of the Line

1920 - 1929:	Szinvavölgyi Erdei Vasút (SzEV)
1929:	Lillafüredi Állami Erdei Vasút (LÁEV)

Company Name

1920 - 1949:	MÁLLERD
1949 - 1991:	ÁEV
1991:	Észak-Magyarországi Erdőgazdasági Rt

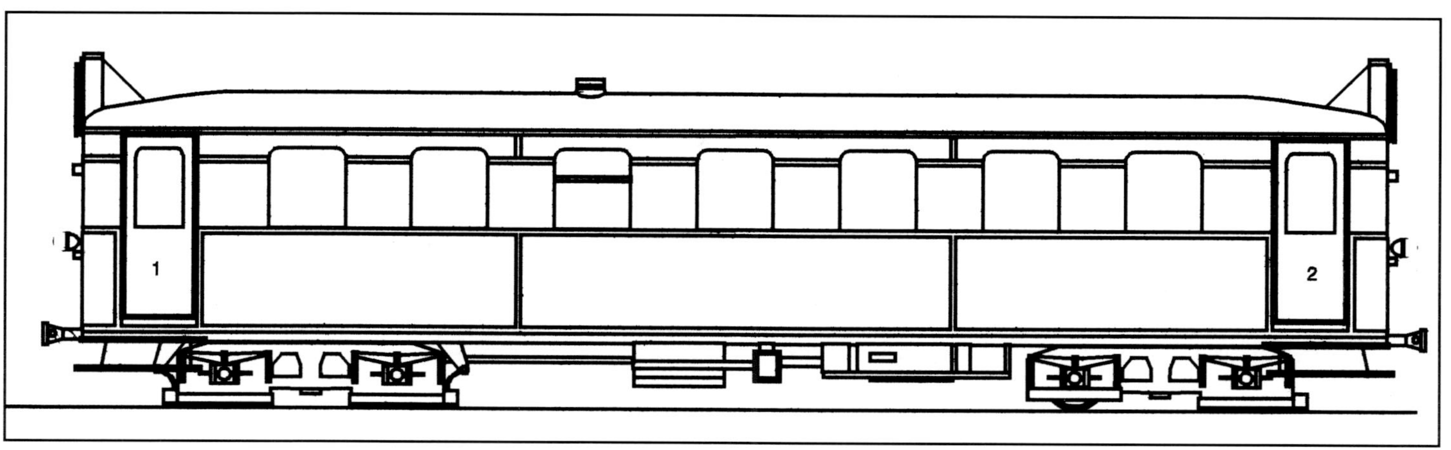

Camot numbers 1 and 2 of the Lillafüred Forestry Railway

Locomotives of the Lillafüred Forestry Railway

Number(s)	Manufacturer	Class	In Service	Remarks
1; 437,401	Bp (4724/1919)	0-8-0T (85)	1922-1960s	ex-GEV 4'; to Felsőtárkány
2; 437,402	Bp (4725/1919)	0-8-0T (85)	1922-1966	ex-FGV III (not used in Hronec)
3; 437,405	Bp (4753/1921)	0-8-0T (85)	1922-?	ex-Hegyközi Vasút 1
4; 437,403	Bp (4726/1919)	0-8-0T (85)	1929-?	ex-Visegrád mine
5; 437,404	Bp (4727/1919)	0-8-0T (85)	1929-1951	ex-Galgamácsa 3; to Gyöngyös
6	Bp (3163/1914)	0-8-0T (70)	1920-1942	ex-MÁV 490,030; to Teresva
357,306	O&K (8435/1917)	0-6-0T	1920-?	ex-Süttő; ex-DHF 504
437,407	O&K (5694/1912)	0-8-0T	? -1948	ex-CGV 3; to Szilvásvárad
447,401	Bp (7254/1954)	0-8-0 (135)	1954-1972	monument at Majláth; restoration started 1996
467,601	Bp (5279/1942)	0-8-0T (70)	1945-1972	ex-Vişeu de Sus 5
467,601	Bp (5850/1950)	0-8-0T (70)	1950-?	to MÁV 490,058
467,602	Bp (5280/1942)	0-8-0T (70)	1945-1960s	ex-Vişeu de Sus 6
C02-402	Éfm (../1955)	C50	? - ?	to Felsőtárkány
M5; C02-405	Éfm (../1960)	C50	1960-1996	
M6; C02-406	Éfm (../1963)	C50	1963-1980	
M7; C02-407	Éfm (../1963)	C50	1963-now	
M10	Éfm (../1954)	C50	1954-1962	to Gyöngyös
M11; C02-411	Éfm (../1954)	C50	1954-1995	
M13; C02-404	Éfm (../1955)	C50	1967-1973	ex-GV 3744; to Felsőtárkány
M492,001	Rába (001/1958)	M040	1959-1960	to Gyöngyös
M492,002	Rába (002/1958)	M040	1959-1960	MÁV Mk48,1012
D02-501	Rába (050/1961)	M041	1977-now	ex-MÁV Mk48,2027
D02-503	Rába (003/1959)	M040	1973-1980s	ex-MÁV Mk48,1003
D02-504	Rába (008/1959)	M040	1973-1980s	ex-MÁV Mk48,1001
D02-505	Rába (011/1959)	M040	1976-1980s	ex-MÁV Mk48,1008
D02-506	Rába (020/1960)	M041	1977-now	ex-MÁV Mk48,2010
M8; D02-508	Rába (033/1961)	M041	1961-now	
D02-510	Rába (034/1961)	M041	1977-now	ex-MÁV Mk48,2011
61101	LOWA (../1953)	Ns3	1962-?	ex-GV 61101
ABmot1; A02-601	Ganz (78950/1929)	B'2'	1929-1980	ran in Budapest 1949 - 1963
ABmot2; A02-602	Ganz (78951/1929)	B'2'	1929-1992	ran on Budapest pioneer railway 1951 - 1963 and from 1996 up till the present.

On 12th July 1996 this typically east European railcar was seen at Majláth motive power depot.
Photo: Paul Engelbert.

This page shows three views of a freight train on the Farkasgödör branch.

Our first sight of D02-508 is at Ortás-tető station.

Photo: Paul Engelbert.

The powerful class Mk48 diesel has difficulties with its short but heavy train on the steep gradients near Andókút.

Photo: Paul Engelbert.

D02-508 shunts empty and loaded freight wagons at Majláth.

Photo: Paul Engelbert.

The Felsőtárkány Forestry Railway

The Eger Archiepiscopal Estate in the Bükk mountains was covered with beech forests, but the transport of timber from the forests to the sawmill at Felsőtárkány was very difficult due to the poor condition of the forest roads and the absence of railways. Therefore in 1915 the Eger Archiepiscopal Estate built a forestry railway from Felsőtárkány to Kisnádas and Petres. The line was horse worked and had a gauge of 760 mm. The depot was situated at Felsőtárkány.

After the First World War the economy and with it the timber trade boomed. In 1922 the Kromberger Mátyás enterprise and the Társai company erected a barrel factory at Felsőtárkány, which used timber from the Eger Archiepiscopal Estate. Of course the logs were transported to the factory by the forestry railway.

Because of the increased demand for timber the forestry railway was extended to Esztáz-kő and at the same time two branch lines to Egeresvölgy-Vöröskővölgy and Öldalvölgy-Határlápa were opened. Határlápa was the starting point of a cable railway and a horse worked economy railway known as the circle railway. During this period the connection between Felsőtárkány and the MÁV railway station at Felnemét was also established and was soon extended to the sawmill in the nearby town of Eger.

After the network was extended the freight volume increased rapidly, amounting to some 200,000 cubic metres of timber transported annually by rail in the late 1920s. By this time the railway was using steam engines instead of horses and traffic continued around the clock. Because of a lack of motive power the loaded trains were often rolled down the hill from Felsőtárkány to Eger without a locomotive, just with some brakesmen on the wagons. As the brakesmen could not always stop the freewheeling wagons in time many accidents happened. The accidents and the continuous noise of wagons rolling through the village of Felsőtárkány did not make the railway very popular with the local population.

After a number of wagons had run into a herd of cows in the streets of Felsőtárkány in 1925, the furious population tore up the railway track in the village, cutting off the forestry railway from the MÁV standard gauge railway station. The line was replaced on a new alignment which ran around the village instead of right through it. In order to resume railway traffic as soon as possible, 500 soldiers helped to build the new line. During the 1930s trains carried more and more limestone, charcoal and above all stone to the MÁV railway station, therefore new branches were opened to a quarry near Berva (1938) and into the Mellér valley (1942).

In 1944 the retreating German army caused a great deal of damage to Hungarian railways and rolling stock was transported westwards or simply blown up. One or more locomotives of the Felsőtárkány forestry railway were hidden in the forests to protect them from the Germans.

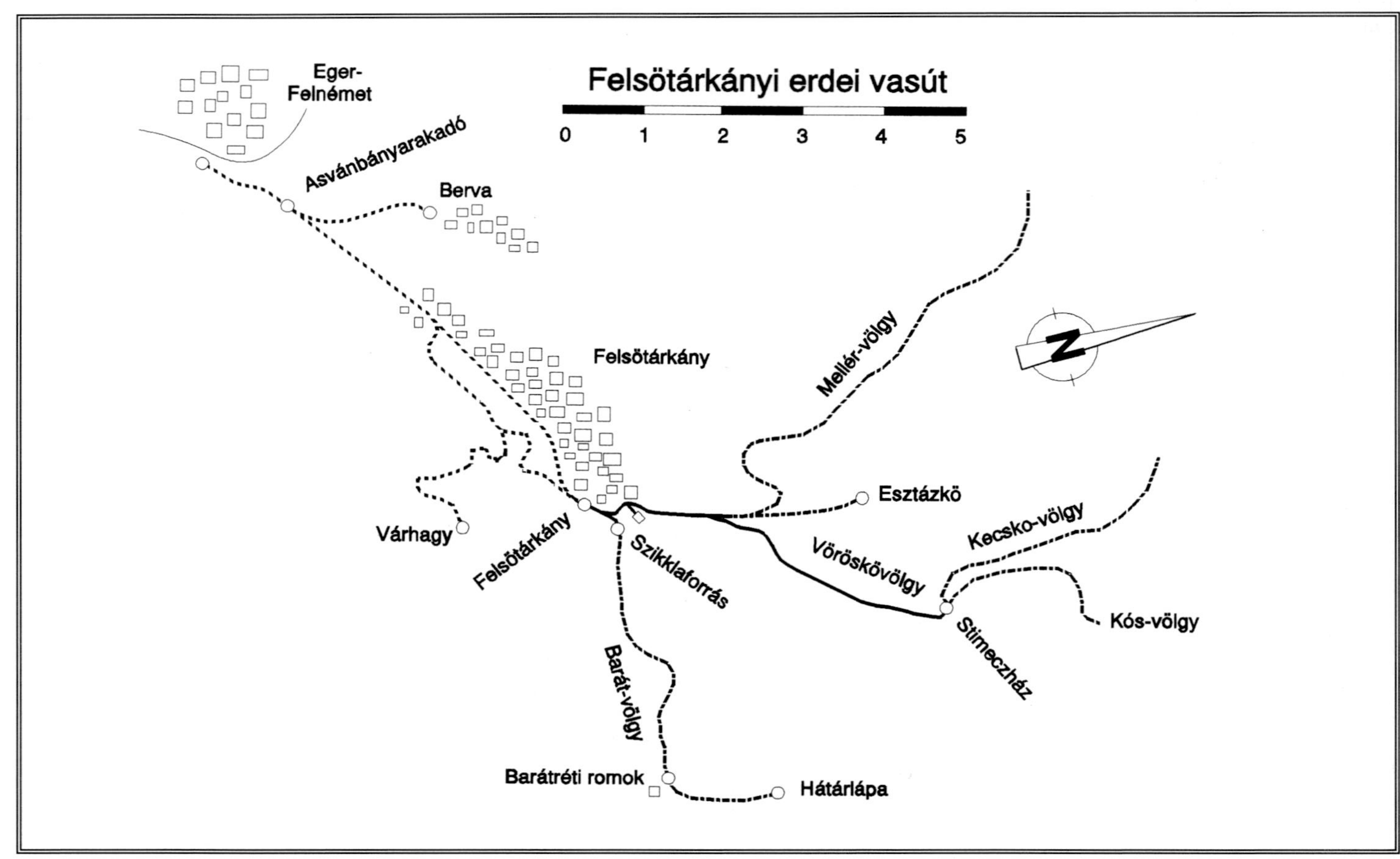

The Felsőtárkány Forestry Railway was steam worked until the mid 1960s, so when ÁEV 357,310 was photographed at Felsőtárkány on 20th August 1958, dieselisation was still a few years away. This locomotive was one of the few built by Arnold Jung to run on a Hungarian Forestry Railway.
Photo: Lászó Mohay.

After the Second World War timber traffic became less important and the line from Felnemét to the sawmill at Eger was closed in 1949. As the freight volume continued to decrease the curtain also fell for the branch lines to Barátrét, Petres and the Mellér valley. Despite the critical situation with timber traffic, the existence of the whole network was by no means in danger as the freight volume on the Berva branch had increased to 5,000 or 6,000 tons of stone every day. The Berva quarry had become the railway's most important customer, earning three million Forints annually. Unfortunately the important stone transport ended in 1964 after the quarry erected a cableway between Berva and Felnemét.

Freight services almost came to an end altogether, but in 1969 a new line was built to the recently opened Várhegy quarry. Every year the railway carried between 45,000 and 50,000 tons of dolomite to Felnemét, from where it was transported on the standard gauge by the MÁV to the iron works at Ózd in northern Hungary. The transport of dolomite continued until 1985.

By that time only 25 kilometres of the original 30 km long network still remained and these lines were almost exclusively used by just a few passenger trains. The passenger service started in 1953 and originally the trains were only used by miners who worked at the Berva quarry, but later many tourists took to travelling on the forestry railway for a visit to the Bükk mountains. Although in 1985 approximately 100,000 passengers used the trains, the passenger service did not bring in enough money to maintain the old track, which was in a very poor condition by that time. As a result 80% of the network was closed by the end of 1985 and passenger trains continued in service only on the remaining 5 km section between Felsőtárkány and Stimeczház. Furthermore the trains only ran from the beginning of May until the end of September. In 1997 just 7000 tourists used the forestry railway.

The lines to Várhegy and to Felnemét were finally lifted in the early 1990s. The former ÁEV station building at Felnemét is still used as the office of the Felnemét timber storage depot and is a reminder of the once important Felsőtárkány - Felnemét forestry railway.

Rolling Stock

All the Felsőtárkány Forestry Railway's steam locomotives were bought second hand. Two locos came from the Austro-Hungarian military railways (kkHB class RIIIc), and the remainder from other industrial or forestry railways. As freight volumes had increased after the Second World War the steam engines were replaced from the 1960s onwards by class C50 diesel engines. These diesels were originally painted dark green but around 1995 the remaining three locos received a bright red livery. In the same year the railway's line number was changed from 03 to 04 and the engines were consequently renumbered. A LOWA Ns3 diesel loco arrived at Felsőtárkány in March 1962, but was diverted to Szilvásvárad in 1963, probably because of its weight.

The passenger coaches stationed at Felsőtárkány are among the most interesting of all forestry railways' stock and these wooden four-axle cars are kept in excellent condition. Many lorries and freight wagons are also retained in the depot at Felsőtárkány, some of them available for special trains.

Company Name

1915 - 1945:	Egri Erseki Uradalom
1945 - 1949:	MÁLLERD
1949 - 1992:	ÁEV
1992:	Mátra-Nyugatbükki Erdő- és Fafeldolgozó Rt.

Name of the Line

1915 - 1945:	Felsőtárkány Erdei Vasút
1949:	Felsőtárkány Állami Erdei Vasút

Locomotives of the Felsőtárkány Forestry Railway

Number(s)	Manufacturer	Class	In Service	Remarks
357,307	Flor (2577/1918)	0-6-0T	1920s-1960s	ex-kkHB RIIIc 149
357,308	Flor (2578/1918)	0-6-0T	? -1960s	from Szilvásvárad
357,309	Jung (2833/1918)	0-6-0T	? -1964	ex-Szár Ilona
357,310	Jung (2836/1920)	0-6-0T	1949-1965	ex-Eger sawmill Erma
427,401	Bp (4724/1919)	0-8-0T	1960s-1966	ex-LÁEV 437,401
M1; C03-401	Efm (../1960)	C50	1960-1986	to Várpalota
M2; C03-402	Éfm (../1960)	C50	1960-1966	to ÁEV Csömödér (III)
C03-402'	Éfm (271/1963)	C50	1982-1986	from Gyöngyös; to Várpalota
C03-402"	Éfm (../1955)	C50	? -1994	ex-LÁEV C02-402; to Pálháza
M3	LOWA (../1953)	Ns3	1962-1963	ex-GV 61103; to Szilvásvárad
M4; C03-403	Éfm (../1962)	C50	1962-now	in 1995 renumbered C04-403
M5; C03-404	Éfm (../1963)	C50	1963-now	in 1995 renumbered C04-404
C03-405	Éfm (../1955)	C50	1973-?	ex-LÁEV M13; to Várpalota
C03-406; C04-406	Éfm (../1954)	C50	1954-now	1964-1982 as MÁEV C05-406

The Felsőtárkány depot is situated in a lovely forestry area just east of the village.
Photo: Paul Engelbert.

When seen on 5th July 1998 the former station building of Felnémet was still in use, though no longer by the ÁEV.
Photo: Paul Engelbert.

On 6th June 1998 Chikán Gábor photographed two trains at Stimeczház, the nearest one headed by C04-403.

688

520 Felnémet—Berva kőbánya

520 521

Valamennyi vonat 2. osztályú kocsikkal (Keskenynyomközű vasút)

					344		338	Km	Állami Erdei Vasutak	339		335					
..	..	..	..	..	⚒14 25	..	⚒22 40	0	i. Berva kőbánya .... é.	⚒ 5 30	..	⚒13 45	..	..	..	..	
..	..	..	..	..	(14 35	..	(22 50	1	Berva gyártelep	(5 20	..	(13 35	..	..	..	..	
..	..	..	..	..	⚒14 40	..	⚒22 55	4	Ásványbányarakodó	⚒ 5 15	..	⚒13 30	..	..	..	..	..

521 Felnémet—Felsőtárkány—Barátréti romok

Valamennyi vonat 2. osztályú kocsikkal (Keskenynyomközű vasút)

	112 ◆	34 ◆	44	36 ◆	38 ◆	48 ◆	138	Km	Állami Erdei Vasutak	39 ◆	49 ◆	35 ◆	45 ◆	13	31 ◆	
..	7 30	13 50	..	..	18 40	20 44	..		i. Eger .... 89 é.	..	6 48	..	15 07	18 35	21 25	..
..	7 50	14 12	..	..	18 59	21 02	..		é. Felnémet .... i.	..	6 29	..	14 47	18 07	21 07	..
..	3 50	12 07	..	..	15 28	..	..		i. Putnok .... 89 é.	..	10 25	..	17 22	21 57	23 20	..
..	6 28	14 46	..	..	18 06	..	..		é. Felnémet .... i.	..	7 56	..	14 13	19 00	21 03	..
..	8 00	14 50	..	..	+ 19 00	+ 21 10	..	0	i. Felnémet .... é.	..	6 17	..	14 30	+17 55	+ 20 50	
..	..	..	⚒14 45	..	..	..	..		Ásványbánya rakodó fmh.	⚒ 5 15	..	⚒13 30	..	..	..	..
..	8 10	15 00	14 55	..	19 10	21 20	⚒ 22 55	4	Felsőtárkány Mészégető	5 05	6 07	13 20	14 20	17 45	20 40	..
..	8 15	15 05	15 00	..	19 15	21 25	23 05	5	Felsőtárkány Dohánygyári üdülő ..	5 00	6 00	13 15	14 15	17 40	20 25	..
..	8 20	15 10	15 05	..	19 20	21 30	23 10	6	Felsőtárkány Vadaskert	4 55	5 50	13 10	14 10	17 35	20 30	..
..	8 25	15 20	⚒15 15	+16 55	19 25	+ 21 35	23 15	7	Felsőtárkány Fűtőház	⚒ 4 45	5 45	⚒13 00	14 00	17 25	20 20	..
..	8 30	15 25	..	16 25	+ 19 30	..	⚒ 23 20	8	Felsőtárkány Sziklaforrás	--	--	..	13 55	17 20	+ 20 15	..
..	8 40	..	..	+17 05	..	..	..	11	é. Barátréti romok .... i.	..	..	..	..	+17 10	..	..

◆ 112, 34, 45 és 49 **Közlekedik:** hétfőn, pénteken
12, 31, 45. 49, 34, 36, 38, 48, 42 **Közlekedik:** IX. 30-ig munkaszünetes napokon

Felvilágosítást ad: Erdőgazdaság Eger. Tel.: Eger 11-30 és Felsőtarkány 3.

An extract from the 1963/1964 timetable shows the passenger train workings on the lines from Felnémet to Berva and to Felsőtárkány and Barátréti, plus connections on the main line.

The Szilvásvárad Forestry Railway

The small village of Szilvásvárad is situated in the Bükk mountains, between Eger and Ózd. Plans for a forestry railway in the area had already been developed by the turn of the century with the intention that the railway should start at the timber storage depot in Szilvásvárad and open up the forests in the Szalajka valley and on the Bükk plateau (Bükkfensík). The first short section of the Szilvásvárad Forestry Railway was built in 1908 by Veszely Károly to a gauge of 600 mm.

Shortly after the end of the First World War the railway was extended. The first new section opened to traffic in 1920 and soon afterwards the network reached it's maximum length of 22 kilometres.

The railway consisted of two separate networks connected by an inclined plane 468 metres long, called the 'siklópálya', necessary to overcome a difference in height of more than 200 metres. The lower part of the network, known as the Szalajkavölgy Erdei Vasút, had gradients of up to six percent, though the upper part, the Bükkfensíki Erdei Vasút, was less spectacular because it traversed the relatively flat Bükk plateau.

The forestry railway of Szilvásvárad was specifically built for the transport of timber felled on the Bükk plateau. The operating method was to carry the wagons of a timber train coming from the plateau down on the inclined plane, and these were then collected from the lower end by a steam locomotive and hauled to the nearby Szilvásvárad timber storage depot. Here the timber was later loaded onto MÁV standard gauge goods wagons.

On the other line, which ran through the Szalajka valley, the trains mainly carried limestone from the Máriabánya quarry at Istállóskő, to Szilvásvárad. Limestone was transported from the mine to the narrow gauge railway by means of a cable railway.

In 1948 the whole network was regauged from 600 mm to 760 mm, making it possible to use heavier rolling stock, enabling freight to be transported in a more efficient way. The railway never really benefited from this improvement though because in 1949 a new road was built which traversed the Bükk plateau and soon road vehicles instead of the forestry railway carried the timber from the forests to Szilvásvárad. Transporting the timber by train was very inefficient in any case as the timber wagons had to be brought down via the inclined plane one at a time.

The Bükkfensíki Erdei Vasút and the inclined plane were probably closed around 1960 but at least the inclined plane was kept as a technical relic and therefore can still be admired. The line from Szalajka-halastó to the lower station of the inclined plane also still exists but cannot be used any more. Mineral trains from the limestone quarry at Istállóskő continued to run after the timber traffic had come to an end, but when the quarry was closed in 1967 the railway lost its last customer.

The Szalajkavölgy Erdei Vasút was not closed, however, because a passenger service, which started in 1953, remained on the 4.5 km long section between Szilvásvárad and Istállóskő-Ősemberbarlang. The passenger trains nowadays are used solely by tourists visiting the Bükk mountain area and the prehistoric caves at Istállóskő, therefore they only run from the beginning of April

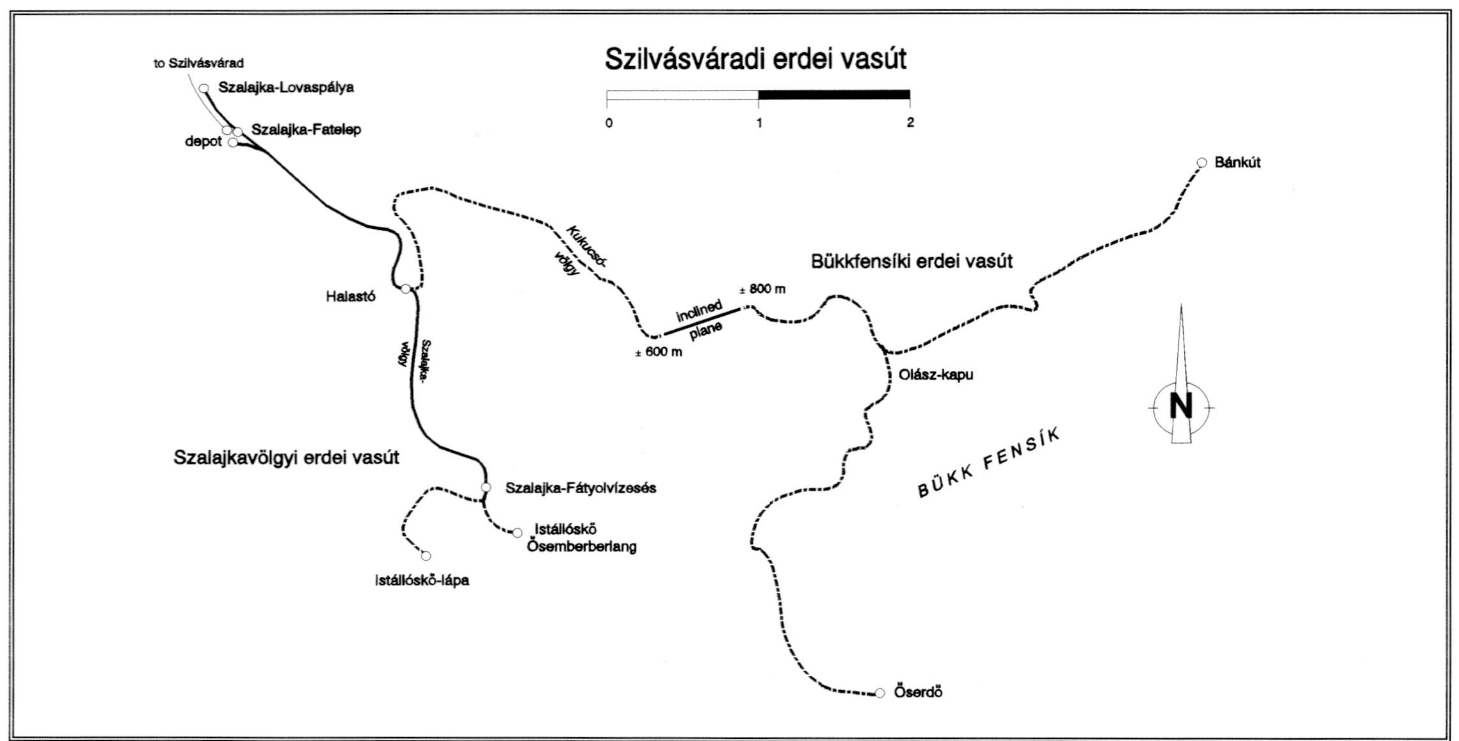

Though already forty years old, ÁEV 0-6-0T 357,301 was regauged from 600 mm to 760 mm in 1948. Fourteen years later, on 1st July 1962, the locomotive was still in a relatively good condition.
Photo: László Mohay.

0-4-0T 257,501 was also regauged to 760 mm. On 31st July 1962, when 59 years old, she was photographed with a passenger train to Szilvásvárad.
Photo: László Mohay.

until the end of October.

After freight traffic had ended the line was operated as a pioneer railway, but unlike some other forestry railways the Szilvásvárad concern was never officially given pioneer railway status. In the late 1960s the station master of Szilvásvárad and the conductors are reported to have been teenagers dressed in pioneer uniforms and the only adult personnel on the railway were the engine drivers. Still, the small trains of this pioneer forestry railway carried a large number of passengers - in 1967 there were 32,000. In 1971 no less than 71,919 passengers travelled on the trains, and by the end of 1981 this number had tripled.

After the end of the 1979 tourist season the section of approximately 800 metres between Szalajka-Fátyolvízesés and Istállóskő-Ösemberberlang was closed. The remaining track, almost four kilometres in length, was completely renewed during the winter of 1979-1980, and in 1984 the station building at Szalajka-fatelep was also renewed, followed by the depot two years later.

Nowadays the line flourishes because Szilvásvárad has become internationally well-known to tourists and in 1997 no less than 193,000 passengers were counted. In 1999, after 30 years of only diesel traction, steam is due to be re-introduced. By using steam traction instead of diesel the management of the railway hopes to attract even more tourists to Szilvásvárad than in the past years.

Rolling Stock

Originally the railway was horse worked but in 1908 a Maffei-built steam locomotive was introduced. Later, as the railway acquired more steam engines, the horses were retired. Like on all other forestry railways, the ÁEV introduced diesel traction, replacing steam, and the last steam engine is presumed to have run in 1967.

Surprisingly, the Szilvásvárad Forestry Railway never used class C50 diesel engines as the 50 HP C50 are not powerful enough to master the steep gradients. In the early 1960s two East German LOWA Ns3 class diesel engines were stationed in Szilvásvárad. The 80 HP Ns3 have a weight of 11 tons, sufficient under normal conditions to prevent the wheels from slipping on the gradients (a C50 only weighs 7 tons). Although the small two-axle Ns3 class diesel engines still needed 25 minutes for the steep uphill 4.5 kilometre drive from Szilvásvárad to Istállóskő, they were more than twice as fast as the steam engines that had been used before. Both of these diesels are members of a series of five Ns3 which were delivered to the GV in 1953, but they are hardly recognisable as class Ns3 because externally they have been fully rebuilt. The original cabs for instance, were replaced by somewhat enlarged cabs as per the class C50 diesel engines.

In the late 1970s the railway acquired two second-hand class Mk48 (Rába type M041), and these powerful four-axle locomotives had almost no problems with the steep gradients. One class Ns3 is still stationed at Szilvásvárad, however, it is only used if both class Mk48 are out of service due to repairs. In 1994 the other class Ns3 went to the narrow gauge museum in Kecskemét and Mk48,2004 was brought to Szilvásvárad to supply spare parts for her two sister engines.

The most recent acquisition is a steam loco, 394,057 (Bp 5785/1949). This Budapest type 106 0-6-0T was bought from the the Nagycenk Museum Railway in 1997 and was expected to be restored to working order by the end of 1998. The loco previously ran on the Taktaharkány - Megyaszó economy railway and at the Sürdokpöspüki mine.

Six closed passenger coaches are used in the spring and autumn, but on hot, and above all, dry summer days open coaches are used. These panoramic summer coaches are reconstructed freight wagons.

Company Name

1920:	Egri Erseki Uradalom
1945 - 1949:	MÁLLERD
1949 - 1991:	ÁEV
1991:	Mátra-Nyugatbükki Erdő- és Fafeldolgozó Rt.

Name of the Line

1920 - 1949:	Szilvásváradi Erdei Vasút
1949:	Szilvásváradi Állami Erdei Vasút

Locomotives of the Szilvásvárad Forestry Railway

Number(s)	Manufacturer	Class	In Service	Remarks
"Csillag"; 257,501	Borsig (5274/1903)	0-4-0T	1920-1960s	
"Eleonóra"; 357,301	Maff (2908/1908)	0-6-0T	1908-1967	
357,308	Flor (2578/1918)	0-6-0T	? -?	ex-kkHB RIIIc 150; to FÁEV
394,057	Bp (5785/1949)	0-6-0T (106)	1998-now	from Nagycenk museum rly
437,407	O&K (5694/1912)	0-8-0T	1948-1960s	from LÁEV
D04,601	LOWA (../1953)	Ns3	1963-1994	ex-FÁEV M3; to Kecskemét
D04,602	LOWA (7451/1953)	Ns3	1965-now	ex-GV 61105
Mk48,403	Rába (019/1960)	M041	1977-now	ex-MÁV Mk48,2007
Mk48,404	Rába (060/1961)	M041	1980-now	ex-MÁV Mk48,2037

25

522 Szilvásvárad—Szalajkavölgy—Istállóskő

Valamennyi vonat 2. osztályú kocsikkal | **Keskenynyomköző vasút**

								Km		Állami Erdei Vasutak									
..	..	4 40	7 30	..	13 50	18 42	..		i.	Eger } 89	é.	6 45	..	15 05	..	18 36	18 48	21 42	..
..	..	6 06	9 13	..	15 35	20 19	..		é.	Szilvásvárad } 89	i.	5 21	..	13 45	..	17 14	17 45	20 20	..
..	..	3 50	6 48	..	12 07	15 28	15 28		i.	Putnok } 89	é.	7 27	10 17	..	17 25	..	..	21 37	..
..	..	5 20	8 22	..	13 44	17 14	17 11		é.	Szilvásvárad } 89	i.	6 07	9 13	..	15 36	..	..	20 08	..
		12 ◆	22 ◆	32 ◆	34 ◆	18 ◆							17 ◆	27 ◆	35 ◆	13 ◆		11 ◆	
..	..	6 50	9 45	11 45	15 10	18 00	..	0	i.	**Szilvásvárad-Örömed**	é.	..	8 10	11 05	13 05	16 30	..	19 20	..
..	..	7 00	9 55	11 55	15 20	18 10	..	2		Szalajka-Halastó		..	8 00	10 55	12 55	16 20	..	19 10	..
..	..	7 25	10 20	12 20	15 45	18 35	..	3		Szalajka-Fátyolvízesés		..	7 50	10 45	12 45	16 10	..	19 00	..
..	..	7 35	10 30	12 30	15 55	18 45	..	4	é.	**Istállóskő-Ősemberbarlang feljáró**	i.	..	7 45	10 40	12 40	16 05	..	18 55	..

◆ A 12, 32, 18, 17, 35, 11 ***Közlekedik:*** munkaszüneti napokon IX. 20-ig
A 22, 34, 27, 13 ***Közlekedik:*** IX. 30-ig naponta,
Menetrendi felvilágosítást ad: Szilvásvárad. Vasútüzem: **Telefon 6**
Erdőgazdaság, Eger. Telefon: 11-30

The timetable from 1st June 1975 to 29th May 1976

The station of Szalajka-fatelep is situated at the foot of the high mountains that surround the Szalajka valley.
Photo: Paul Engelbert

D04-601 is preserved together with the former Szilvásvárad buffet coach at the narrow gauge railway museum near the station at Kecskemét KK, where this photo was taken on 16th July 1996.
Photo: Paul Engelbert.

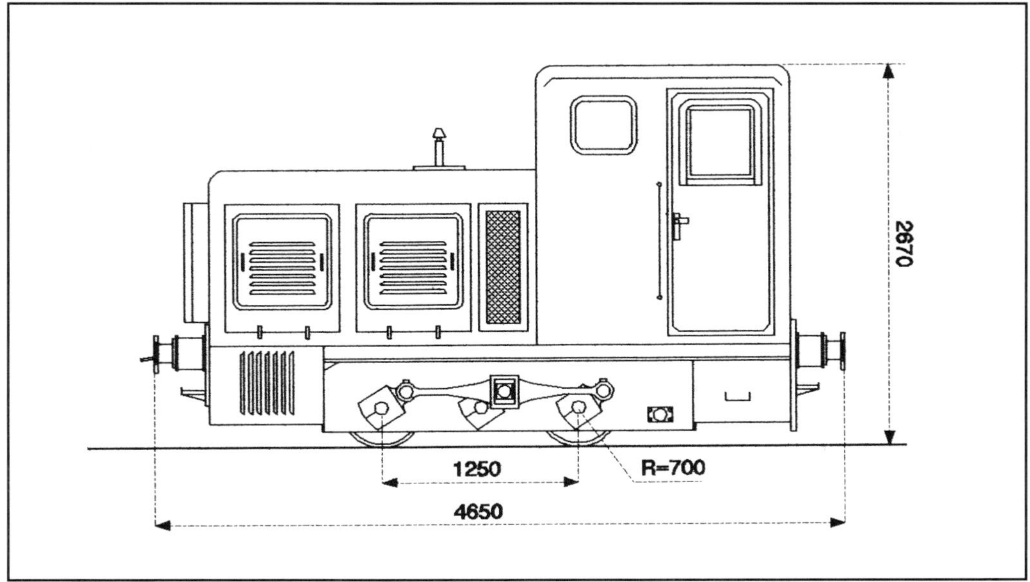

The reconstructed LOWA Ns3 of the ÁEV

The Gyöngyös Forestry Railway

The Mátra mountain area in northern Hungary has summits of between 600 and 700 metres. The region is covered with oak forests and the mountains are rich in minerals, however, the extraction of all these natural supplies was very difficult because of the limited transport facilities in the Mátra region.

In 1870 the town of Gyöngyös, which is situated some five kilometres south of the Mátra mountains, gained a connection to the national railway system. In the following decades many plans for an extension of this standard gauge railway into the Mátra mountains were developed. Plans presented ranged from a short electric railway to Mátrafüred to a proposal for a standard gauge railway to the town of Bánréve, traversing the complete mountain area. None of these projects were realised and the economic development of the region stagnated. In order to alleviate the transport problems local companies built their own private railways. Two of them, the Gyöngyössolymos Forestry Railway and the Farkasmály Economy Railway, formed the basis of the present day Gyöngyös Forestry Railway.

The Gyöngyössolymos Forestry Railway was built by a corporation formed by the Eger Archiepiscopal Estate and the Mátra Timber Trading Company. In 1906 it laid a 600 mm gauge line from Lajosháza to Gyöngyössolymos, where there was a small depot. In 1907 the railway was extended from Lájosháza to Szalajkaház, followed by a branch line from Gyöngyössolymos into the Monoster valley in 1914. The forestry railway reached a length of approximately 27 kilometres and had no connection to the national railway network. The line was used for the transportation of both timber and minerals.

The Gyöngyössolymos line was horse worked until a small steam engine named 'Liza' arrived in September 1915. Her journey to the depot in Gyöngyssolymos may not be left unmentioned. Because there was no railway connecting Gyöngyös and Gyöngyössolymos the locomotive had to run the last six kilometres on her own. To prevent the heavy engine from subsiding into the sandy roads a temporary railway had to be built between both stations. In order to minimize the costs it was decided to use just a short section of portable track which had to be dismantled after the 'Liza' had passed and put together in front of the loco again, each time making it possible to roll a few metres further.

The Farkasmály Economy Railway was built in 1911, again by the Eger Archiepiscopal Estate, this time in a corporation with the Barna-féle Company. The 3.4 km long 600 mm gauge railway connected the Farkasmály quarry to the MÁV railway station in Gyöngyös. The line was steam worked and had a depot in Gyöngyös.

In 1917 both railway systems were connected by a five kilometre line from Gyöngyös to Gyöngyössolymos. The next year the Gyöngyös - Farkasmály line was extended to Mátrafüred by the town of Gyöngyös, but due to reforms and economic problems caused by the end of the First World War the opening of this new section was postponed until 1923.

The combined railways, which now had a total length of some 38

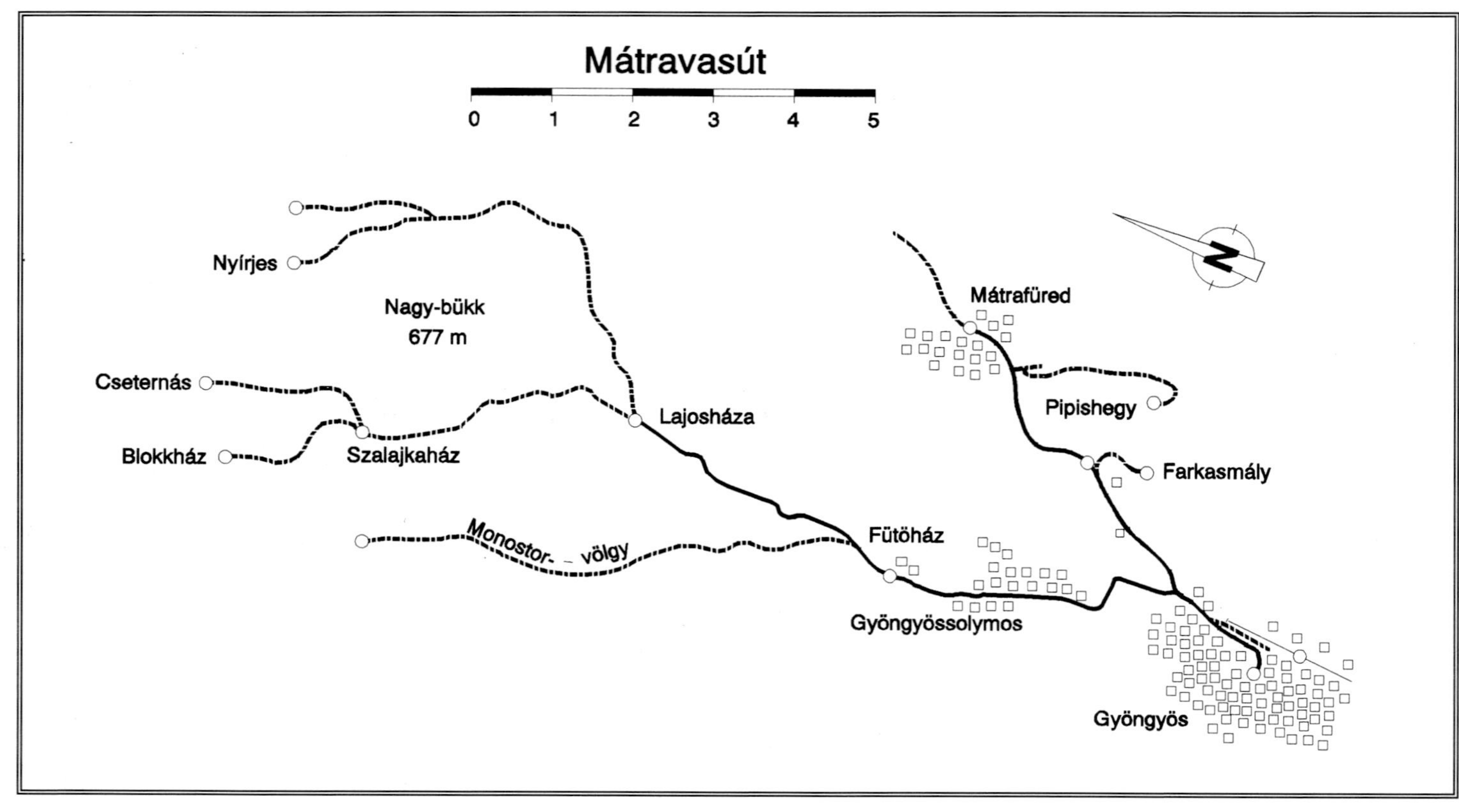

In the 1930s open passenger coaches were used on the line to Mátrafűred. The locomotive in this old postcard view is 'Karcsi', fitted with a strange swan neck chimney as a spark arrestor. Photo courtesy of the Közlekdési Muzeum, Budapest.

kilometres, flourished and traffic increased rapidly. Therefore in 1925 the track was completely renewed and on this occasion also regauged from 600 mm to 760 mm, making it possible to use heavier rolling stock than before.

Until the network was regauged the railway was only used for freight traffic, but in 1926 a passenger service was started on the 5.4 kilometer long section between Gyöngyös and Mátrafüred. The trains were mainly used by tourists and therefore only ran from April till October. The service proved to be a great success and in the first season 8,000 passengers used the trains. Ten years later this number had already increased to approximately 40,000.

During the Second World War traffic continued normally but in November 1944 the front reached the Mátra area and traffic had to be suspended. It took a year before the first freight trains ran again on the Mátra Forestry Railway. The passenger service to Mátrafüred was resumed in 1947.

In 1945 the communist government nationalised the Eger Archiepiscopal Estate. Afterwards the Gyöngyössolymos Forestry Railway, which was situated in the archiepiscopal estate, came under the administration of the Hungarian state forestry company MÁLLERD. The Farkasmály Economy Railway, however, was owned and operated by the town of Gyöngyös and therefore was not nationalised in 1945. Since 1949 both the Gyöngyössolymos Forestry Railway and the Farkasmály Economy Railway have been administered by the ÁEV, ending the somewhat strange situation of a forestry railway operated by two separate companies.

In the 1950s the ÁEV played an important role in the succesful industrialisation of the Mátra region. New companies settled alongside the narrow gauge railway and transport volumes increased drastically. In 1951 a new 3.6 km long branch line was

On 5th July 1994 Mk48,409 crosses a small bridge near Gyöngyös felső. The passenger coach was still in the light blue livery of the MÁV narrow gauge network south of Kecskemét.
Photo: Paul Engelbert.

437,404, a Budapest type 85, was transferred from Lillafüred to Gyöngyös in 1951. On 11th October 1959 this lovely engine was photographed in Gyöngyös.
Photo: László Mohay.

'Muki' was the first steam loco on the Farkasmály economy railway. Numbered 437,408 the old 'Muki' was still used for passenger trains in 1957, as seen here at Gyöngyös on 15th September of that year.
Photo: László Mohay

opened to a new factory at Pipishegy and in 1961 the scheduled passenger service on the Gyöngyös - Lajosháza section started. In the heyday of the Gyöngyös Forestry Railway there were at times no less than 14 pairs of freight trains and 6 pairs of passenger trains a day running on a network just 46 km long.

On 28 May 1961 the Gyöngyös Forestry Railway was officially given pioneer railway status. The freight traffic continued, making the Gyöngyos forestry railway probably the only official pioneer railway with both scheduled passenger and freight trains.

In 1961 the railway carried 160,000 tons of freight and 400,000 passengers, however, in the late 1960s and 1970s freight traffic became ever more insignificant. In 1966 the trains still carried 101,220 tons of timber, but in 1976 only 13,682 tons remained. Two years later the transport of timber came to a complete end. The railway not only lost the timber traffic but also the other freight traffic and in 1980 the last train carrying stone arrived in Gyöngyös. The remaining freight traffic finally ended in 1984 and many lines were closed. Only the lines from Gyöngyös to Lajosháza and to Mátrafüred, which were still used for passenger traffic, remained open. Eventually the network was reduced to a length of just 18.5 km.

Contrary to the freight traffic, passenger traffic flourished. Every year more people travelled on the trains. In the peak year of 1976 the railway carried 555,410 passengers but after 1976 the numbers dropped quickly. In 1978 a mere 289,815 passengers were counted and in 1987 the railway lost its status as a pioneer railway. At that time only some 200,000 passengers patronised the Mátra Forestry Railway.

After the iron curtain had ceased to exist the situation became precarious because the number of passengers kept dropping and the losses were no longer compensated for automatically by the government. Over 1991 the railway had a deficit of 4.5 million Forints (at that time approximately £30,000) and was balanced on the edge of a financial crisis. Fortunately the local and national governments and regional commerce and industry prevented the closure of the Mátra Forestry Railway, so nowadays one can still enjoy a trip by train to Mátrafüred or Lajosháza. In 1997 133,660 passengers travelled on the Mátravasút.

The Mátrafüred line is quite special because it is the only line on which a passenger service is operated that is really of importance for the local population and not just for tourists. Inhabitants of Mátrafüred mainly use the railway as a means to reach the MÁV railway station in Gyöngyös and for shopping trips. Trains run the whole year round on workdays and also from April until October at weekends. Unfortunately the line lies immediately beneath a broad asphalt road, through which most of the charm of this forestry railway fades away.

The layout of the line to Lájosháza is much more picturesque. After the line has branched away from the route to Mátrafüred an agricultural area is traversed. About two kilometres further the railway reaches a small river, which it follows until reaching the village of Gyöngyössolymos. The curvy track making its way through the winding sandy streets of Gyöngyssolymos is probably the most interesting feature of the line. But also the sand dunes north of the former depot (Fűtőház) at Gyöngyössolymos, the enormous buildings of the former stone loading berth at Őrlőmű and the final two kilometres through a narrow river valley are very impressive too.

Although the trains are used by the local population, most passengers now are tourists visiting the Mátra mountain area. Therefore the trains only run during the tourist season from May until

The last active class C50 is hardly used any more. On 7th July 1995 Jörg Körner photographed C50,404 with just one open summer coach at Lajosháza.

The enormous buildings at Örlőmű are reminders of the intensive freight traffic in the 1960s and 1970s.
Photo: Paul Engelbert.

September at weekends, and on Wednesdays and Fridays in June and July.

Rolling Stock

Three steam locomotives were stationed on the Farkasmály Economy Railway, for use on the passenger trains and for hauling freight trains. The Gyöngyössolymos Forestry Railway only had one steam engine at his disposal. Only after both railways had been taken over by the ÁEV did a fifth steam engine come to Gyöngyös.

Since 1953 the Mátra railway has used diesel engines, which gradually replaced all the steam locomotives. The last scheduled steam train ran in 1964, by which time a total of six class C50 were stationed in Gyöngyös. In 1960 a powerful diesel mechanical class Mk48 also came to the line for trial runs, but in 1963 the loco returned to the MÁV, who used the engine on one of its own narrow gauge local railways.

After the MÁV had closed many of these local lines in the late 1970s and had started to dump many of the now redundant class Mk48, the ÁEV bought four of these engines for the Gyöngyös Forestry Railway. These Mk48, which have a diesel hydraulic driving unit, are still in service whilst most class C50 were withdrawn in the late 1970s or early 1980s.

During the 1970s and 1980s the ÁEV also bought modern four-axle passenger coaches from the MÁV These carriages, originally green, brown or blue are now all painted bright red with yellow stripes. Apart from the closed passenger coaches there are also three open summer coaches, one of which is a former closed passenger coach and the other two rebuilt from freight wagons. There are only a few freight wagons left in working order, used for maintenance trains. Many more rust-eaten wagons remain at the former Gyöngyössolymos depot.

Locomotives of the Gyöngyös Forestry Railway

Number(s)	Manufacturer	Class	In Service	Remarks
Karcsi	WrN (../1918)	0-6-0T	1923-1943	ex-kkHB RIIIc; to Csömöder
337,301 'Gizi'	Bp (4761/1924)	0-6-0T (99)	1929-1941	to Takcsány
357,303 'Liza'	Bp (3790/1915)	0-6-0T (107)	1915-1967	originally Gyöngyössolymos
437,404 'Kékes'	Bp (4727/1919)	0-8-0T (85)	1951-1959	ex-LÁEV 5
437,408 'Muki'	O&K (5108/1911)	0-8-0T	1911-1959	
M12; C05-401	Éfm (141/1953)	C50	1953-1979	to ÁEV Lenti
M13; C05-402	Éfm (211/1954)	C50	1954-1979	to ÁEV Lenti
M14; C05-403	Éfm (168/1954)	C50	1954-1970s	
M15; C05-404	Éfm (../1954)	C50	1962-now	
M16; C05-405	Éfm (271/1963)	C50	1963-1982	to ÁEV Felsőtárkány
M17; C05-406	Éfm (../1954)	C50	1964-1982	from Berva; to Felsőtárkány
Mk48,409	Rába (057/1961)	M041	1976-now	ex-MÁV Mk48,2034
Mk48,410	Rába (058/1961)	M041	1976-now	ex-MÁV Mk48,2035
Mk48,411	Rába (018/1961)	M041	1977-now	ex-MÁV Mk48,2005
Mk48,412	Rába (055/1961)	M041	1980-now	ex-MÁV Mk48,2032
Mk48,1011	Rába (001/1958)	M040	1960-1963	from LÁEV; to MÁV

Companies of the Gyöngyössolymos Line

1906 - 1945:	Egri Erseki Uradalom & Mátrai fakitermelésre alapított Rt.
1945 - 1949:	MÁLLERD
1949 - 1992:	ÁEV
1992:	Mátrai Erdő- és Fafeldolgozo Gazdaság Rt.

Name of the Gyöngyössolymos Line

1906 - 1949:	Gyöngyössolymosi Erdei Vasút
1949 - 1961:	Mátravasút (Gyöngyösi Állami Erdei Vasút)
1961 - 1987:	Mátrai Úttörővasút - Gyöngyös
1987:	Mátravasút (Gyöngyösi Állami Erdei Vasút)

Companies of the Farkasmály Line

1911 - 1932:	Gyöngyös - Benei Vasút Rt
1926 - 1932:	Gyöngyös Megyei Város Villamosműve (passenger service only)
1932 - 1944:	Mátravasút
1944 - 1949:	Gyöngyös Város Közművei
1949 - 1992:	ÁEV
1992:	Mátrai Erdő- és Fafeldolgozó Gazdaság Rt.

Name of the Farkasmály Line

1906 - 1932:	Benei Vasút
1932 - 1961:	Mátravasút (Gyöngyösi Állami Erdei Vasút)
1961 - 1987:	Mátrai Úttörővasút - Gyöngyös
1987:	Mátravasút (Gyöngyösi Állami Erdei Vasút)

On 29th June 1997 the silence in the quiet streets of Gyöngyössolymos is briefly disturbed by the passenger train from Lajosháza to Gyöngyös. Photo: Paul Engelbert.

Below: The timetable of the Mátra Pioneer Railway from 1st June 1975 until 29th May 1976.

524 Gyöngyös–Gyöngyössolymos–Lajosháza

Valamennyi vonat 2. osztályú kocsikkal közlekedik — **Keskenynyomközű vasút**

Km	Állami Erdei Vasutak Mátrai Úttörővasút		212 ◆	222 ◆		232 ◆	210 ◆		214 ◆	224 ◆		236 ◆	246 ◆			
0	**Gyöngyös-Előre** ind.	..	7 52	9 30	..	11 10	11 10	..	13 12	14 40	..	16 04	17 36	..	..	..
1	Gyöngyös-Pajtás	..	7 54	9 32	..	11 12	11 12	..	13 14	14 42	..	16 06	17 38	..	..	..
3	Jánoska	..	8 04	9 42	..	11 22	11 22	..	13 24	14 52	..	16 16	17 48	..	..	..
5	Zemanek	..	8 11	9 49	..	11 29	11 29	..	13 31	14 59	..	16 23	17 55	..	..	..
6	**Gyöngyössolymos**	..	8 14	9 52	..	11 32	11 32	..	13 34	15 02	..	16 26	17 58	..	..	..
9	Őrlőmű	..	8 23	10 01	..	11 41	..	..	13 43	15 11	..	16 35	18 07	..	..	..
11	**Lajosháza** érk.	..	8 28	10 06	..	11 46	..	..	13 48	15 16	..	16 40	18 12	..	..	..

524 Lajosháza–Gyöngyössolymos–Gyöngyös

Km	Állami Erdei Vasutak Mátrai Úttörővasút		207 ◆	217 ◆		227 ◆	235 ◆		215 ◆	223 ◆		233 ◆	241 ◆			
0	**Lajosháza** ind.	..	..	8 42	..	10 20	11 54	..	13 52	15 22	..	16 50	18 22	..	..	..
2	Őrlőmű	..	..	8 47	..	10 25	11 59	..	13 57	15 27	..	16 55	18 27	..	..	..
5	**Gyöngyössolymos**	..	..	8 56	..	10 34	12 08	..	14 06	15 36	..	17 04	18 36	..	..	..
6	Zemanek	..	6 08	8 59	..	10 37	12 11	..	14 09	15 39	..	17 07	18 39	..	..	..
8	Jánoska	..	6 15	9 06	..	10 44	12 18	..	14 16	15 46	..	17 14	18 46	..	..	..
10	Gyöngyös-Pajtás	..	6 25	9 16	..	10 54	12 28	..	14 26	15 56	..	17 24	18 56	..	..	..
11	**Gyöngyös-Előre** érk.	..	6 27	9 18	..	10 56	12 30	..	14 28	15 58	..	17 26	18 58	..	..	..

◆ 212, 217 **Közlekedik:** V. 1-től IX. 30-ig munkaszünetes és azt megelőző munkanapon
207 **Közlekedik:** szerdán és pénteken
222, 232, 214, 224, 236, 246, 227, 235, 215, 223, 233, 241 **Közlekedik:** V. 1-től IX. 30-ig
212, 222, 210, 217, 227, 235 **Közlekedik:** X. 1-től IV. 30-ig szerdán és pénteken Gyöngyössolymosig

525 Gyöngyös–Mátrafüred

Valamennyi vonat 2. osztályú kocsikkal közlekedik — **Keskenynyomközű Vasút**

Km	Állami Erdei Vasutak	110	112 ◆	122 ◆	132 ◆	142 ◆	142b ◆	114 ◆	124 ◆	116 ◆	126 ◆	118 ◆	128 ◆	138 ◆		
0	**Gyöngyös-Előre** ind.	✕ 5 40	6 50	7 50	8 50	10 00	11 00	12 00	14 00	15 00	16 40	17 50	18 50	20 00	..	..
1	Gyöngyös-Pajtás	5 42	6 52	7 52	8 52	10 02	11 02	12 02	14 02	15 02	16 42	17 52	18 52	20 02	..	..
3	Farkasmály-Borpincék	5 48	6 58	7 58	8 58	10 08	11 08	12 08	14 08	15 08	16 48	17 58	18 58	20 08	..	..
5	Pipishegy	5 53	7 03	8 03	9 03	10 13	11 13	12 13	14 13	15 13	16 53	18 03	19 03	20 13	..	..
6	Mátrafüred-Kozmáry	5 58	7 08	8 08	9 08	10 18	11 18	12 18	14 18	15 18	16 58	18 08	19 08	20 18	..	..
7	**Mátrafüred** érk.	✕ 6 00	7 10	8 10	9 10	10 20	11 20	12 20	14 20	15 20	17 00	18 10	19 10	20 20	..	..

The Királyrét Forestry Railway

North of Budapest the River Danube flows by the Börzsöny mountains. More than a century ago a Prussian count, who owned a large part of the forests in this area, built a forestry railway there. The 11.5 kilometre long line started in Kismaros, a small village on the northern shore of the River Danube, and ran via Királyrét to a timber loading point at Adolfkút. The 600 mm gauge railway was steam worked.

In 1912 two branch lines were opened, from Királyrét to quarries at Cseresznyefa and Bajdázó. Because timber and stone cannot be loaded onto standard gauge railway wagons at Kismaros a further branch was built to the next standard gauge station at Verőce. After another short branch had been built from Kismaros to the banks of the Danube it also became possible to transfer the timber to river transport in the small port at Kismaros.

Paphegy became the centre of the enlarged forestry railway network and a new depot, a workshop, a stonemill and an electricity plant for the mines were erected there. After the network had been extended the volume of freight increased rapidly. Every day at Verőce between 60 and 70 standard gauge wagons were loaded with timber and stone brought in by forestry railway and six new steam locomotives were needed to haul the many heavy freight trains.

The forestry estate changed ownership twice after the First World War and the final owner, a Swissman called Hoffer, continued to exploit the rich mineral supplies in the Börzsöny mountains until 1941. In that year all the quarries were closed and the railway lost most of its freight, however, the line remained open because it continued to transport timber. The freight volume dropped to between 5000 and 6000 cubic metres of timber per annum and a number of steam engines were withdrawn.

In 1945 the private forestry estate was nationalised. The quarries were reopened and the railway started carrying stone to Verőce station again. Furthermore, the main line was extended from Királyrét to a timber loading point at Egyházbükk where about 20,000 cubic metres of timber were loaded onto the narrow gauge trains annually. In the 1950s the quarries were closed again. By that time the line to Egyházbükk had fallen out of use, so the once important freight traffic was now reduced to an occasional timber train running from the loading point at Cseresznyefa to Verőce.

If these timber trains had been the only source of income for the railway it would have been be closed by now for sure, but since 26 May 1954 a public passenger service has been operated between Kismaros and Királyrét. In the early 1960s the passenger trains also ran from Királyrét to Nagyhideghegy (Cseresznyefa) and Csóványos (Egyházbükk).

On workdays many of Szokolya's residents who worked in Budapest used the passenger trains to travel to Kismaros and from here the standard gauge commuter trains of the MÁV brought them into Budapest. On Sundays day-trippers from Budapest travelled in the opposite direction. For many years before the start of the public passenger service special passenger trains had been taking children from Királyrét and Paphegy to and from the school in Szokolya and these continued to run.

The public passenger service was an enormous success. In the 1960s up to 600,000 passengers frequented the trains every year. In 1976 the line was officially declared a pioneer railway and a number of stations were renamed. Kismaros became Verőcemaros felső, Hártókút became Krónikás, Paphegy became Kincskereső and Királyrét alsó became Tábortűz. The number of passengers using the pioneer railway kept rising, however, it was impossible to increase the number of trains or to use heavier rolling stock on the

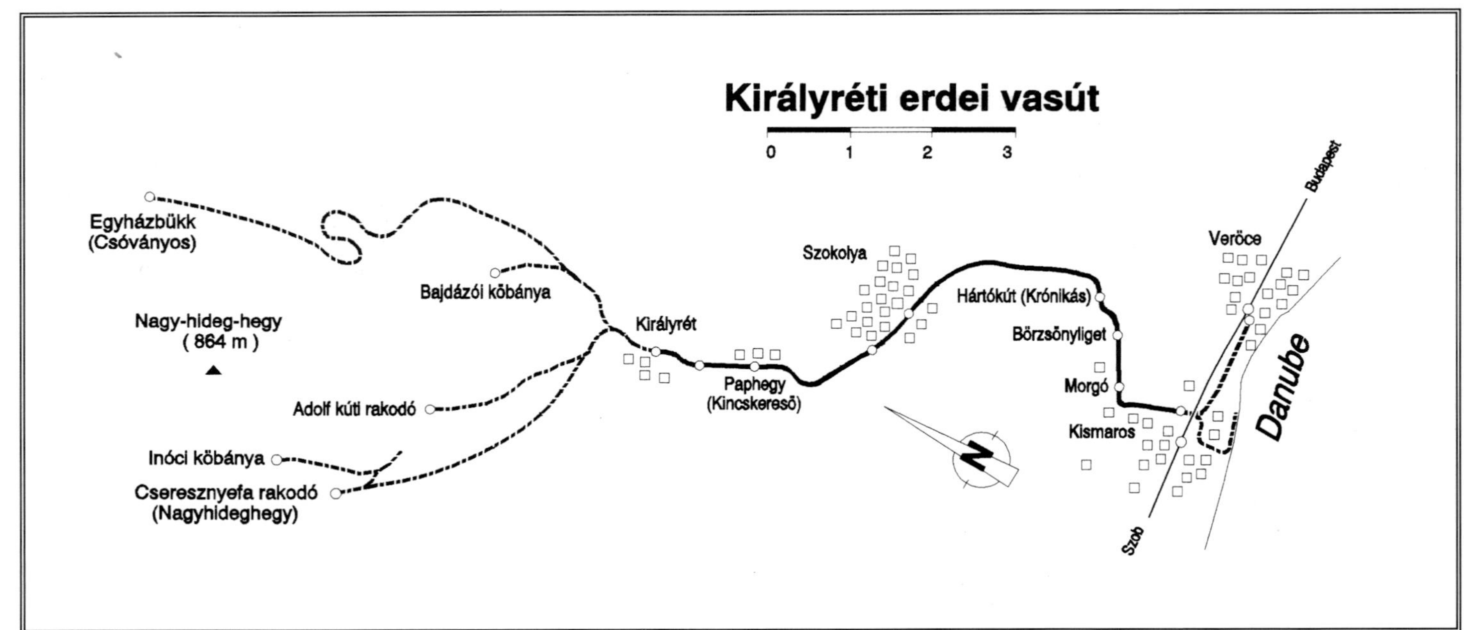

A picture of the scenic Paphegy depot on 10th September 1957. On the left we see 357,301 'Triglav'. This was the last active steam engine of the ÁEV and can now be admired at the Nagycenk museum. The class MD40 diesel, number P2, stands between the steam engines. On the right hand side is 357,306, a former German army locomotive (O&K 8435/1917).
Photo: László Mohay.

600 mm gauge railway, so it was decided to regauge the line to 760 mm.

In 1979 the old 600 mm gauge line from Verőce via Kismaros and Királyrét to the loading point at Cseresznyefa, only occasionally used, was closed. It was two years before traffic was resumed because the track was not only regauged, but also renewed using old 23kg/m rails from the closed standard gauge railway from Cegléd to Hantháza. In the meantime passengers had to travel by bus. The line from Verőce to Királyrét was reopened on 7th June 1981, but the freight-only line from Királyrét to Cseresznyefa was not rebuilt.

After the communist regime fell in 1989 the railway lost most of its passengers. The number of commuters travelling between Szokolya and Budapest had decreased because of sudden high unemployment and those people who were lucky enough to keep their jobs tended more and more to use their cars instead of public transport to get to work. Only at the weekends were trains still busy, as they were quite frequently used by day-trippers. In 1997 only 69,255 passengers travelled on the railway, only one tenth of the passengers carried in the 1960s.

Although the number of trains was reduced and some personnel made redundant, the railway got into financial difficulties. From 1992 rumours about the closure of the railway were in the air and sometimes apparently the trains did not run at all for several days. The line was probably only able to survive by selling off redundant rolling stock, but luckily the situation has improved and trains now run according to the timetable and are well frequented.

Forty years after the photo above, in January 1997, the old buildings and steam engines have been replaced by a modern metal shed and class Mk48 diesel locomotives.
Photo: collection of Paul Engelbert.

In 1957 passenger trains were hauled by class MD40 diesel engines. Photo: Collection of the Közlekedési Múzeum.

517 Kismaros–Királyrét–[Nagyhideghegy / Csóványos]

Valamennyi vonat 2. osztályú kocsikkal — Keskenynyomközű Vasút

Km		i./é.																
	Bpest nyugati pu.	i.	..	5 35	6 40	7 48	..	..	13 11	13 35	..	15 12	15 57	..	17 28	19 19	21 25	..
	Vác	i.	..	6 40	7 50	9 00	..	11 19	13 53	14 21	..	16 23	16 48	..	18 25	20 31	22 31	..
	Kismaros	é.	..	6 58	8 19	9 18	..	11 38	14 16	14 39	..	16 41	17 06	17 44	18 43	20 49	22 49	..
	Szob	i.	4 12		..	.	..	11 34	..	..	..	15 24	..	..	..	..	..	..
	Kismaros	é.	4 50	..	..	..	..	11 59	..	..	16 13	15 59	..	17 44	..	..	..	..
Km	Állami Erdei Vasutak		120	142	122 ◆	132 ◆	144	124	114 ◆	116 ◆	146	136	126	126b	118	138	128	
0	**Kismaros**	i.	⚒ 5 10	7 05	(8 27	(9 23	..	12 10	(14 20	(14 56	+16 14	⚒16 43	⚒17 30	+17 50	18 50	20 55	22 53	..
2	Morgó		(5 17	7 12	(8 34	(9 30	..	12 17	(14 27	(15 03	(16 21	(16 48	(17 37	(17 55	18 57	21 02	23 00	..
3	Börzsönygyöngye		(5 22	7 14	(8 36	(9 32	..	12 19	(14 29	(15 05	(16 23	(16 50	(17 39	(17 57	18 59	21 04	23 02	..
4	Börzsönyliget		(5 25	7 17	(8 39	(9 35	..	12 22	(14 32	(15 08	(16 26	(16 52	(17 42	(18 00	19 02	21 07	23 05	..
5	Hártókút	é.	..	7 21	(8 43	..	..	12 26	..	(15 12	..	..	(17 46	..	..	..	..	..
		i.	..	7 22	(8 44	..	..	12 31	..	(15 13	..	..	(17 48	..	..	..	..	..
7	Szokolya alsó		(5 44	7 35	(8 54	(9 50	..	12 44	(14 49	(15 26	(16 40	(17 01	(18 00	(18 08	19 19	21 24	23 18	..
8	**Szokolya felső**	é.	(5 50	..	..	..	..	12 49	(14 54	..	+16 45	⚒17 05	..	(18 12	..	21 30	..	..
		i.	(5 53	7 40	(8 58	(9 55	⚒ ..	13 10	(14 55	(15 31	..	..	(18 05	(18 13	19 24	..	23 22	..
10	**Paphegy**		(6 01	7 48	(9 06	(10 04	(11 30	13 18	(15 06	(15 41	..	..	(18 15	(18 22	19 32	..	23 30	..
11	Királyrét alsó		(6 04	7 51	(9 09	(10 07	(11 33	13 21	(15 09	(15 45	..	..	(18 18	(18 24	19 34	..	..	..
12	**Királyrét**	é.	⚒ 6 10	7 57	(9 14	(10 13	⚒11 38	13 26	(15 16	(15 50	..	..	⚒18 25	+18 30	19 40	..	..	..
		i.	..	..	(9 18	(10 17	..	..	..	..	..	..	..	..	..	..	..	..
	Nagyhideghegy [3]	é.	..	..	(9 58	..	..	..	..	..	..	..	..	..	..	..	..	..
16	6 **Csóványos**	é.	..	..	..	(11 02	..	..	..	..	..	..	..	..	..	..	..	..

114 ***Közlekedik:*** szombaton, VIII. 18-án, XII. 24-én, IV. 3-án
Nem közlekedik: VIII. 17-én, IV. 4-én és V. 2-án
116 ***Nem közlekedik:*** szombaton
A 122 és 132 sz. vonatok Királyrét–Nagyhideghegy, illetve Királyrét–Csóványos között csak munkaszünetes napokon ***közlekedik:*** IX. 30-ig, valamint III. 31-től

In 1963 passenger trains still ran from Kismaros to Nagyhideghegy (Csoresznyfa) and Csóványos (Egyházbükk).

Rolling Stock

Traffic started in 1893 with a two-axle, wood-fired steam locomotive. Twenty years later many more two-, three- and four-axle steam engines, most of them former German and Austro-Hungarian military locomotives, were stationed on the line. In the late 1920s

Mk48,2031 has just left Kismaros with a passenger train to Királyrét.
Photo: Paul Engelbert, 4th July 1994.

The station of Kismaros on the same day as above. The track in the foreground used to run to Verőce.
Photo: Paul Engelbert.

the railway started to experiment with petrol-driven draisines, but the only one that was really succesful was a Fiat that could carry eight people and was used particularly for the school trains between Királyrét and Szokolya.

In 1962 four class C50 diesel locomotives made the old steam engines redundant. The last active steam locomotive was 'Triglav'. She ran for the last time on 12th September 1972 and was afterwards transported to the narrow gauge railway museum at Nagycenk.

Since the railway was regauged five heavy class Mk48 have hauled the trains. They were bought second-hand from the MÁV and kept their original numbers. In 1994 Mk48.2019 was sold to the Zillertalbahn in Austria and in the same year a French museum railway bought C06-401. The following year the Zillertalbahn also acquired a number of passenger coaches.

Company Name

1893 - 1920:	Gróf Frenkensiesdorf
1920 - 1924:	Bank Jánospusztai Uradalom és Ipartelepek Rt
1924 - 1945:	Királyréti Uradalom és Ipartelepek Rt
1945 - 1949:	MÁLLERD
1949 - 1991:	ÁEV
1991:	Ipoly Erdő Rt

Name of the Line

1893 - 1976:	Királyréti Erdei Vasút
1976 - 1989:	Börzsönyi Úttörővasút
1989:	Királyréti Állami Erdei Vasút

Locomotives of the Királyrét Forestry Railway

Number(s)	Manufacturer	Class	In Service	Remarks
'Sándor'	Jung (173/1893)	0-4-0T	1893-1941	to Borsod mine
'Mária'	Bp (564/1893)	0-4-0T (20)	1941-1943	ex-Baglyasalja Mária
'Triglav'; 4; 356,301	KrMü (4713/1902)	0-6-0T (18ai)	1913-1972	ex-kkHB IIId481; to Nagycenk
'Koblav'; 1	O&K (1260/1904)	0-4-0T	1913-1941	ex-kkHB 870; to Mezőhegyes
'Muki'; 2; 256,001	KrMü (6129/1909)	0-4-0T (27bf)	1912-1955	ex-M&F; to Tokaj
356,401	Bp (2205/1911)	0-6-0T (75)	1950s-?	ex-Hird
3; 356,402	Bp (3272/1914)	0-6-0T (86)	1914-1950s	ran in Hird in early 1950s
'Muki' (357,306)	O&K (8435/1917)	0-6-0T	1918-1962	ex-DHF; to Süttő
'Vilmos'	Hen (14905/1916)	0-8-0T	1918-1941	ex-DHF 936 (Brigadelok)
'Királyréti Hármas'	O&K (5619/1912)	0-6-0T	1955-?	ex-MÁV 396,017
I Trezina	Fiat (215/1939)	draisine	1939-1970s	
P-1	KE (../1948)	MD40	1948-1950s	
P-2	PBJV (45038/1956)	MD40	1956-1979	
M1; C06-401	Éfm (../1959)	C50	1959-1994	to museum railway in France
M2; C06-402	Éfm (../1962)	C50	1962-1979	
M3; C06-403	Éfm (../1964)	C50	1964-1979	
M4; C06-404	Éfm (../1967)	C50	1967-1979	
Mk48,2014	Rába (037/1961)	M041	1981-now	ex-MÁV Mk48,2014
Mk48,2017	Rába (040/1961)	M041	1981-now	ex-MÁV Mk48,2017
Mk48,2018	Rába (041/1961)	M041	1981-now	ex-MÁV Mk48,2018
Mk48,2019	Rába (042/1961)	M041	1981-1994	ex-MÁV; to Zillertalbahn (D7)
Mk48,2031	Rába (054/1961)	M041	1978-now	ex-MÁV Mk48,2031

Mk48,2031 with passenger coach number 01 at Kismaros. This open summer coach was sold to the Zillertalbahn in 1994. Photo: Paul Engelbert.

Lillafüred's Abmot2, the former A02-602 nowadays runs on the Budapest Children's Railway.
Photo: Paul Engelbert.

D02-501 with a passenger train in the lovely station at Majláth on the Lillafüred system in July 1996.
Photo: Paul Engelbert.

On 12th July 1996 D02-508 was photographed with a maintenance train at Mahóca (Lillafüred Forestry Railway). This has been the terminus of the Farkasgödör branch line since approximately 1991.
Photo: Paul Engelbert.

It is not only steam locomotives that are preserved. Szilvásvárad's D04-601 can also now be found in the narrow gauge museum at Kecskemét
Photo: Paul Engelbert.

C50-1 with a passenger train near Bázakerettye on the Csömödér system in July 1996.
Photo: Paul Engelbert.

C50-3 has just left Pördefölde with a freight train to Csömödér on 20th July 1995.
Photo: Paul Engelbert.

The line from Gyöngyös to Mátrafüred mainly runs directly beside the road. At Gyöngyös felső Mk48,411 makes a striking spectacle with its coaches in a matching livery.
Photo: Paul Engelbert.

In 1997 FKG built a new diesel locomotive on the basis of CDH24-404. On 17th July 1997 C50Z-404 was in service at Pörböly on the Gemenc Forestry Railway.
Photo: Roland Beier.

The Lenti Forestry Railway

One of Hungary's least known forestry railways can be found in the Zala district in the south-west of the country. After the First World War or maybe even before, a large sawmill was erected directly south of the Lenti standard gauge railway station. Here the timber from one of the forestry estates of the Esterházy family was processed. The family owned many agricultural and forestry estates in the western part of Hungary, amounting to a total area of approximately 5,000 km^2, and on some of these estates narrow gauge railways were used to transport the timber from the forests to the sawmill. This was the case at Lenti.

The line is known to have remained in private hands until at least 1945 but probably actually until 1949. It could not be confirmed, but all indications are that the forestry railway, which was apparently seen as a part of the sawmill, has been administered by the various national economy railway companies. In 1960 the network was turned once more into an official forestry railway.

The Lenti Forestry Railway consists of two main lines and once had a length of 34.5 km over which the maximum speed was 30 km/h. The 760 mm gauge track was laid with rails of 9 kg/m.

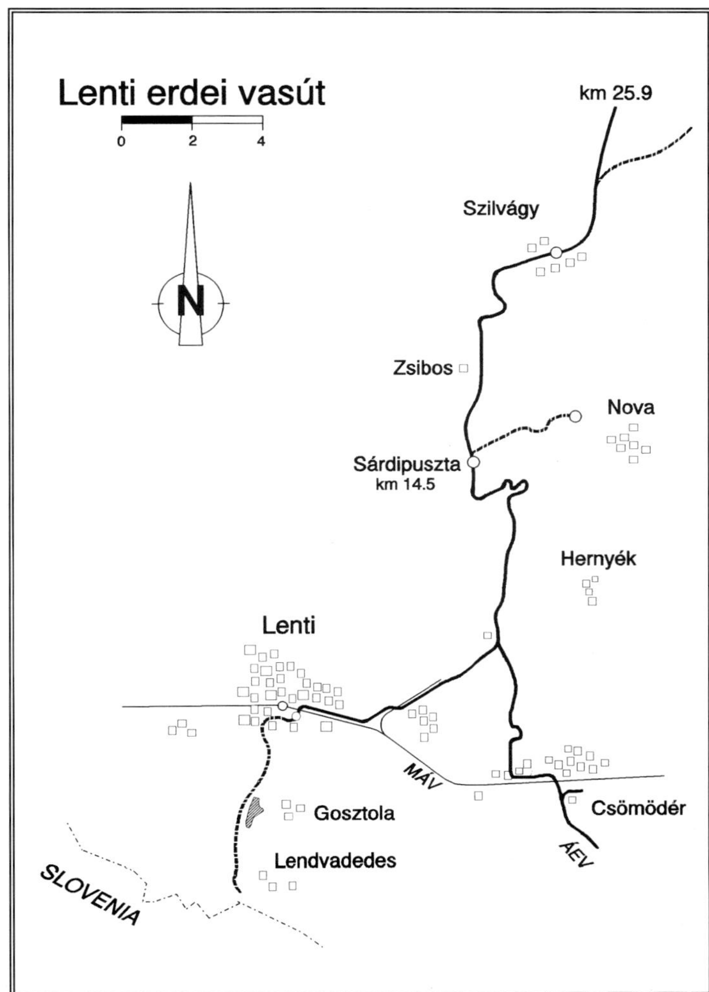

The first section of the northern line was built in 1923 and the last section in 1928. It leaves the sawmill's premises just before passing across the standard gauge railway from Rédics to Zalegerszeg, at which point the railway crossing is secured by a low turnable barrier. The route follows the standard gauge track, until after three kilometers, near the village of Lentiszombathely, it turnes north through the wide and uninhabited valley of the Malonya-patak. In the forests west of the village of Nova there are a few enormous curves after which a small station called Sárdipuszta is reached. It has only two tracks and no station building but it was here that the line to Nova branched off. This branch was opened in 1925 and extended in 1951. From Sárdipuszta the line runs via the settlement of Zsibos to the village of Szilvágy and ends after 25.9 kilometers in the forests north-east of Szilvágy.

The second main line started on the south side of the sawmill. The line terminated after 5.9 km, between the village of Lendvadedes and the present Slovenian and former Jugoslavian border. Whilst the the northern line still exists, the southern line was closed in the 1970s, however, the track was probably only lifted around 1992. Now a three kilometer long section of this former line, just south of Lenti, is in use as a cycle way.

The Lenti narrow gauge station, which consists of two tracks and a small engine shed, is situated on the sawmill's premises. Behind the station the timber can be loaded directly from the narrow gauge onto the standard gauge wagons. The narrow gauge railway station is not easy accessible because it lies behind the fence around the sawmill's premises but whilst the main entrance is guarded, a small gate near the engine shed can be passed without any problems.

Traffic on the forestry railway was probably never very intensive judging by the simple layout of the stations and the rolling stock and for most of the time the line to Szilvágy has only been used occasionally. In 1996, for instance, the trains were only running on the first 17 km section as far as Zsibos. The next year the trains ran through to the terminus north of Szilvágy again and in the summers of 1997 and 1998 the trains were reported to have run every weekday, leaving Lenti around 8 o'clock in the morning and returning around noon again. The trains do not always bring the logs all the way from the forests to the sawmill. It is known that the forestry railway has also been used for the transportation of logs between a cutting area and a loading point for lorries.

Because the line runs through an inaccesible nature reserve, the Lenti forestry railway, unlike many ÁEV lines, never operated a public passenger service despite the fact that the region is well known to tourists. There is even a camping site right in front of the sawmill where the forestry railway begins, yet the only passenger trains are specials run for hunters.

Rolling Stock

During the railway's first years the trains were hauled by a steam loco, 'Antal', a sister of 'Pál' which ran a few kilometres away at Csömödér. It was presumably some years later that another steam loco 'Muki' came to Lenti. The steam engines were replaced in the mid 1960s by class C50 diesel engines and 'Muki' was preserved in front of the office building on the sawmill's premises. The first class C50 was called 'Iván'. Three other class C50s came to Lenti second-hand at a later stage, and two of these are still stationed in Lenti but only number 2 is reported to be operational.

For the transport of timber two trains can be arranged. One consists of bogie freight wagons and the other of small four-wheel bolster wagons. The shunters of the freight trains travel in a home-made coach, but for the occasional passenger trains the Lenti forestry railway acquired a bogie passenger coach. In the 1950s about 100 such coaches were built for the GVI and the one now at Lenti previously ran on the Dombovár network.

Name of the Line

1923 - 1949:	Lenti Erdei Iparvasút
1949 - 1960:	Lenti Gazdasági Vasút
1960:	Lenti Állami Erdei Vasút

Company Name

1923 - 1949:	Esterházy family
1949 - 1955:	Gazdasági Vasútak Nemzeti Vallalat, Kaposvár
1955 - 1960:	GVI
1960 - 1991:	ÁEV
1991:	Zalerdő Rt

On 1st September 1997 a short freight train has just left the Lenti sawmill and is crossing the standard gauge railway. Photo: Helge Ralf Harling.

The crossing of the standard and narrow gauge lines at Lenti is secured by turn-able barriers.

Photo: Paul Engelbert.

Locomotives of the Lenti Forestry Railway

Number(s)	Manufacturer	Class	In Service	Remarks
357,313 'Antál'	O&K (10526/1923)	0-6-0T	1923-1965	
357,305 'Muki'	O&K (8418/1917)	0-6-0T	? - ?	from Csömödér; ex-DHF 487; now preserved at Csömödér.
'Iván'	Éfm (../..)	C50	1950s- ?	
D04-036	Éfm (../1952)	C50	1969- ?	ex-GV 4504 (Újszentmargita)
1 (C14-401)	Éfm (141/1953)	C50	1979-now	ex-ÁEV Gyöngyös M12
2 (C14-402)	Éfm (211/1954)	C50	1979-now	ex-ÁEV Gyöngyös M13

C50 no. 2 shunts empty stock at Sárdi station on 3rd June 1994. Note the locally made coach.
Photo: Jörg Körner.

Trains are sometimes loaded at the small station of Sárdipuszta.
Photo: Helge Ralf Harling.

The Csömödér Forestry Railway

The Csömödér forestry railway was built during the First World War by the forest tenants R. Schäffer and M. Mayer, who exploited the forests in the Count Esterházy estate between Csömödér and Nagykanisza in the Zala district. The 14.8 km long line from Csömödér via Törösnek and Pördefölde to Budnya was commissioned on 15 March 1918 in order to connect the Esterházy forestry estate to the Csömödér sawmill and the railway station. The forestry railway was built to a gauge of 760 mm, laid with rails weighing 7 kg per metre, and was locomotive worked from the beginning.

In the early 1920s another line was opened which ran from Törösnek via Bánokszentgyörgyi and Oltárc to Marki erdő. This route was only commissioned just as the whole railway network was taken over by the Esterházy family on 14 March 1922. In the late 1930s the network was extended. The Kövecses branch line was opened in 1936, followed by the Kistolmács branch line in 1937 and the Bánkütös branch line in 1938. After some additional short branch lines were built the Csömödér Forestry Railway reached its maximum length of approximately 76 km.

Near Páka there was an inclined plane which connected the Csömödér network to the Vétyempuszta forestry railway but after this 7,7 km long network had been closed in 1948 the inclined plane was abandoned.

The Csömödér narrow gauge railway is often the only means of transport in the wide swampy valleys. The lines run through varied countryside, where the track is in many places built on a low dam through marshland. Small forests follow after green meadows, and a steep and winding section can be found in the hills south of Bázakerettye. The Csömödér - Oltárc main line and the Kistolmács branch line run through small villages, whereas the other lines find themselves in almost uninhabited valleys.

Most of the time the logs are loaded onto the wagons at permanent loading points, which can be reached by truck or by tractor. Where there is no seperate loading point the wagons are loaded

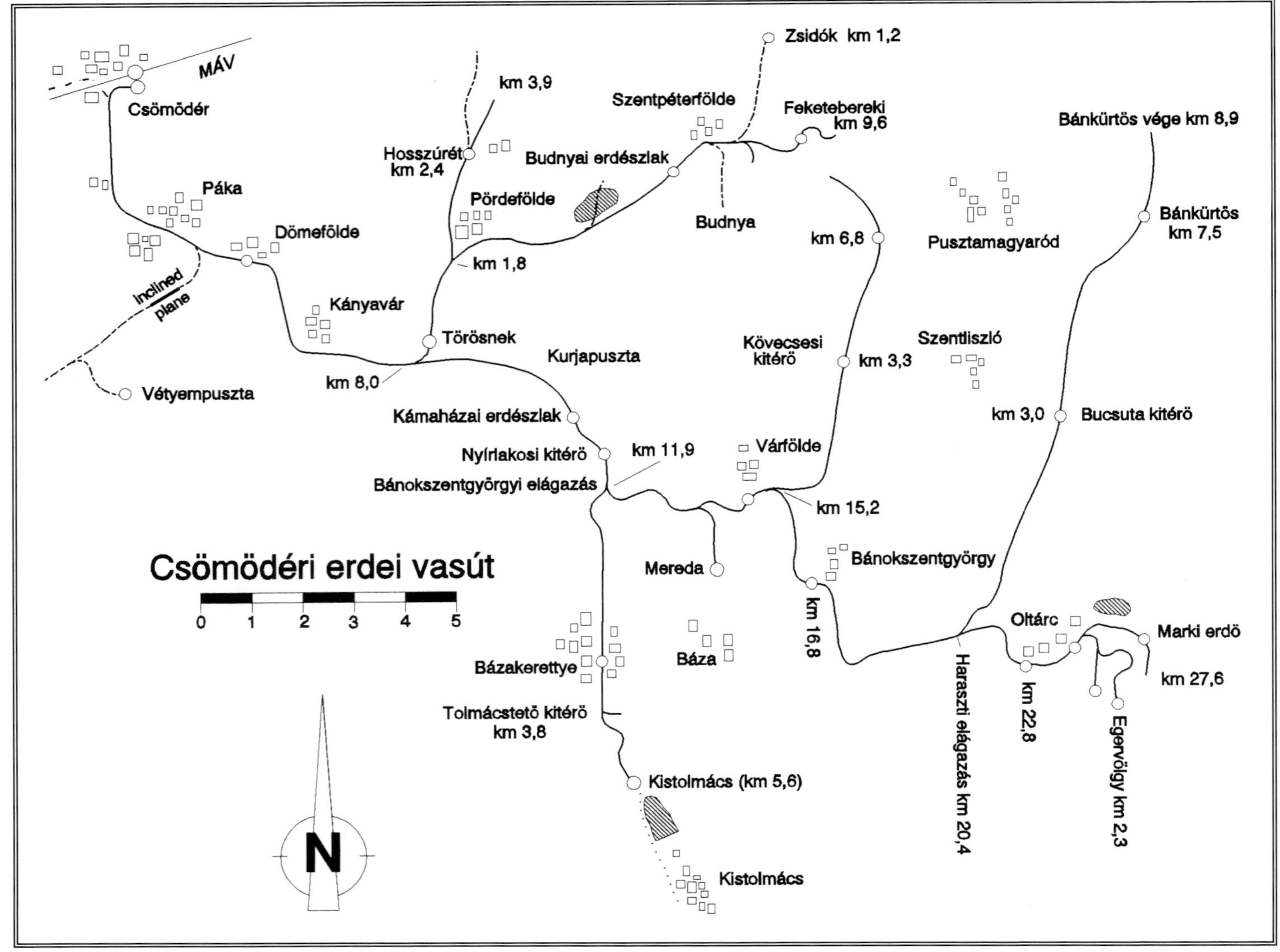

357,314 'Hanyi Istok' was the last steam engine on the Csömödér Forestry Railway. On 7th July 1996 she was photographed at the Nagycenk narrow gauge museum. Photo: Paul Engelbert.

while the train is standing on the main line.

The layout of the few stations, which are only used to pass a train from the opposite direction, is always very simple. Only a handful of them have a small station building. Train crossings can also take place where another line branches off. One of the trains is simply put on a side track or branch line in order to clear the main line for the train from the opposite direction. On the other hand the track layout on the sawmill's premises in Csömödér is very complicated as there are numerous tracks which connect almost every building and storage area. Two tracks are used for loading the logs from the wagons of the narrow gauge railway onto the MÁV standard gauge railway wagons and a two track engine shed is integrated into the sawmill's main building.

Freight traffic on the Csömödér forestry railway is still very intensive with the trains carrying more than 30,000 cubic metres of timber to the Csömödér sawmill every year. From Monday to Friday several trains will be working their way between the loading points and the sawmill. Sometimes a number of trains run to the same loading point but it is also possible that several lines are serviced on the same day. Freight traffic starts between 6 and 7 o'clock in the morning and sometimes ends early, at around noon. The trains are composed of a class C50 and about five bogie freight wagons, although occasionally a passenger train brings a freight wagon to a loading point on the Kistolmács branch line.

The passenger service has existed since 1949. At first the trains ran between Csömödér and Bázakerettye but by 1963 the service had been extended to Kistolmács. On Mondays to Fridays three trains are run between Csömödér and Kistolmács and up until 1990 there was an additional service on Saturdays. Apart from the freight and passenger trains, a maintenance train consisting of some goods wagons carrying materials and a green wagon for personnel is operated almost every day.

The passenger trains depart from the Csömödér sawmill's premises. The quickest way to reach the narrow gauge passenger train when coming from the MÁV railway station is by crossing the MÁV tracks, going through a door in a high fence and again crossing some standard gauge and narrow gauge loading tracks. To get there via the official but much longer way one enters the sawmill's premises on the opposite side.

The manangement of the Csömödér railway has rather spectacular plans for the future. The Zalaerdő company has built a connection between the Csömödér and the Lenti network starting from the Csömödér sawmill. After crossing the standard gauge line the narrow gauge line runs north until it reaches the Lenti - Szilvágy line near Mumor. The new line, which is due to be opened in 1999, makes it possible to run direct freight trains from Szilvágy, Zsibos and Sárdipuszta to the Csömödér sawmill instead of to the Lenti sawmill. The total cost was estimated at 90 million Forints. The combined Csömödér and Lenti networks have a length of 106 kilometres, which makes it the largest narrow gauge network in Hungary at present. Apart from the new line to Lenti the Zalaerdő company also wants to extend the Kistolmács branch line to the village of Kistolmács and maybe later to the town of Letenye, 7 km south of Kistolmács.

Rolling Stock

The first steam engine, named 'Tátra', was ordered by the Prince Frigyes Habsburg forestry estate in Végles (now Viglaš, Slovakia). It was not delivered because Slovakia was seperated from Hungary after WW1 and instead 'Tátra' went to Csömödér. Between the two world wars there were at least four steam locomotives stationed at Csömödér and after the war more steam engines are reported to have run on the network. In the 1960s they were gradually replaced by an ever growing number of class C50, most of them bought second hand from the MÁV GV. The last steam loco, 'Hanyi Istok', ran until 1973, then it went to Nagycenk.

In 1996 the railway bought four scrap C50 with the numbers 5MC4 - 5MC7 from the closed Sárszentmihály industrial railway. Of these locos only 5MC4 was restored to working order again. At the same time twelve freight wagons and two passenger coaches (one Bax and one BDax-type) were bought from the MÁV narrow gauge railway at Nyíregyháza and will be restored in the future.

On 2nd June 1998 Romanian steam engine 764.460 arrived at Csömödér. This locomotive was built by Reşita for the CFF and last ran at Finiş. The engine will have to be restored before it can be used to haul tourist trains at Csömödér and Lenti. The acquisition of one or two class Mk48 diesel engines is to be the next step.

At the Csömödér sawmill the timber can be transhipped onto standard gauge freight wagons as seen here in July 1995.
Photo: Paul Engelbert.

C50-4 had stopped at Páka halt when seen on 19th July 1995.
Photo: Paul Engelbert.

Company Name	
1918 - 1922:	R. Schäffer & M. Mayer
1922 - 1945:	Esterházy Hercegi Hitbizomány
1945 - 1949:	MÁLLERD
1949 - 1991:	ÁEV
1991:	Zalerdő Rt

Name of the Line	
1922 - 1945:	Esterházy Hercegi Hitbizomány Csömödéri Erdei Iparvasút
1945:	Csömödéri Állami Erdei Vasút

Locomotives of the Csömödér Forestry Railway

Number(s)	Manufacturer	Class	In Service	Remarks
764.460	Reş (1199/1956)	0-8-0T	1999?- ?	from CFF Finiş, Romania
'Tátra'	Bp (2198/1910)	0-6-0T (75)	1918 - 1940s	ordered by Véglesi Erdei Vasút
337,301	Bp (4761/1924)	0-6-0T (99)	1945 - ?	from Takcsány
357,305 'Muki'	O&K (8418/1917)	0-6-0T	1922 - ?	ex-DHF 487; to Lenti
357,312 'Pál'	O&K (10525/1923)	0-6-0T	1923 - 1965	
357,314 'Hanyi Istok'	O&K (10726/1923)	0-6-0T	? - 1973	from Lébény (Wenckheim estate); to Nagycenk
357,401	.. (../1909)	0-6-0T	1923 - 1959	
Karcsi	WrN (../1918)	0-6-0T	1943 - ?	from Gyöngyös
I; D04-007	Éfm (../1959)	C50	1959 - now	
II; E04-029	Éfm (../1963)	C50	1963 - now	
III	Éfm (../1960)	C50	1966 - now	ex-ÁEV Felsőtárkány C03-402
4	Éfm (../1955)	C50	1980 - now	ex-GV 3760 (Dombovár)
5	Éfm (../1952)	C50	1980 - now	ex-GV 3704 (Dombovár)
M2001 (6)	Éfm (../1952)	C50	1988 - now	ex-GV 3707 (Dombovár)
M2002 (7)	Éfm (../1955)	C50	1989 - now	ex-GV 3769 (Dombovár)
(8)	Éfm (../1952)	C50	1996 - now	ex-Sárszentmihály 5MC4

C50 no. 1 hauls a full load of timber over the level crossing at Oltárc on 2nd September 1997.
Photo: Helge Ralf Harling.

C50-5 with five freight wagons at the loading point in Kámáházi erdészlak on 10th July 1996.

Photo: Paul Engelbert.

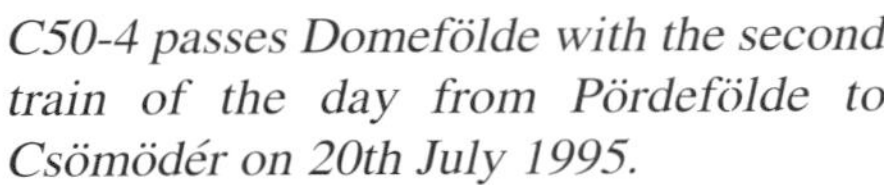

C50-4 passes Domeföld with the second train of the day from Pördeföld to Csömödér on 20th July 1995.

Photo: Paul Engelbert.

M2001 stands in front of the engine shed at Csömödér. This loco and sister engine M2002 are only used to shunt on the sawmill's premises.

Photo: Paul Engelbert.

The Kaszó Forestry Railway

The landscape in the Somogy district in south-west Hungary is mainly flat agricultural country with some forests. One of the most extensive wooded areas in this district is the Kaszó forestry land, with many hectares of oak and alder forest. In the 1920s a forestry railway approximately 10 km long connecting the MÁV railway station in Somogyszob with the forests around Kaszó already existed. In the beginning the line was worked with horse traction but during the 1930s a steam engine hauled the timber trains, however, the line was probably destroyed in 1944 by the retreating German army.

After the Second World War the original forestry railway was not reopened. Instead a new line was planned which did not start at the MÁV railway station in Somogyszob but in Szenta. North of Szenta railway station there was a small sawmill where the timber could be procesed before further transportation by standard gauge train. The railway was built with 9.3 kg per metre rails and a gauge of 760 mm. Work started in 1952 and in 1955 the main line about 12 km long from Szenta to Rinya and the 2 km branch line to Kaszó were opened to traffic by the ÁEV. Later other branch lines were built, extending the network to a total length of around 30 km. A small engine shed was erected in Kaszópuszta.

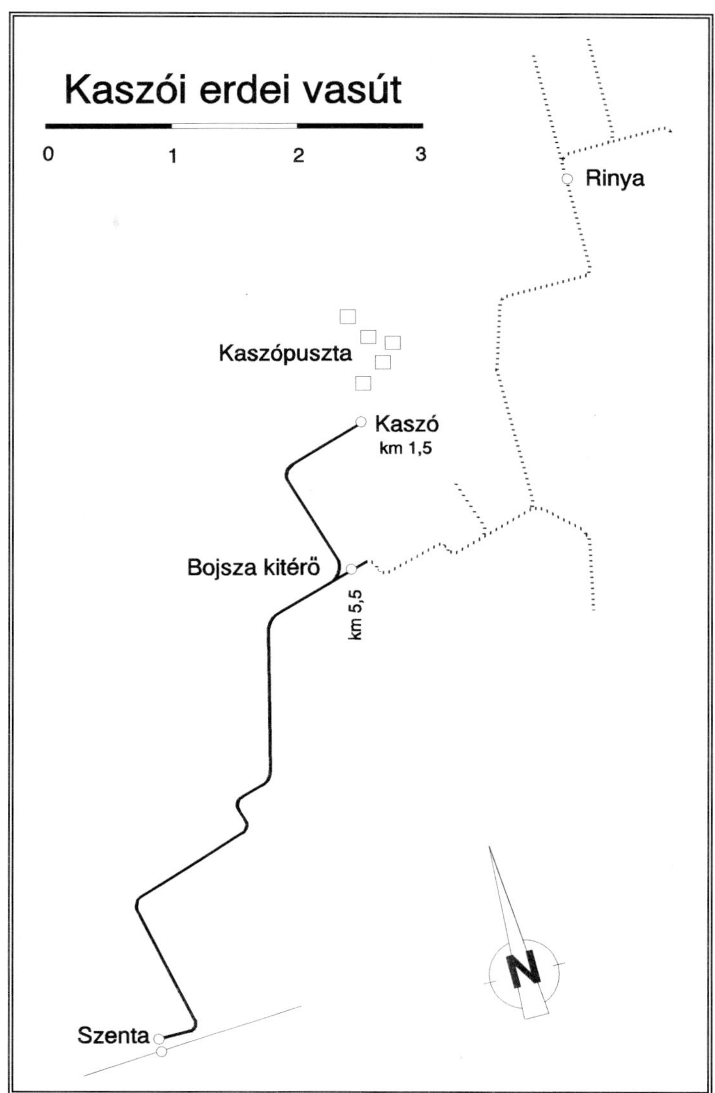

Initially the forestry railway was only used for freight traffic. The trains carried on average about 12,000 cubic metres of timber and a few tons of other, mainly agricultural, products each year. The scheduled passenger service on the main line to Rinya and the branch line to Kaszó started in 1961. After the main line had been extended from Rinya to Nagyrinya puszta in 1963, the passenger trains also ran to Nagyrinya puszta, however, the passenger traffic was never of great importance as on average only a few dozen people a day used the trains.

In the 1960s the Kaszó forestry concern built many forest roads which could be used by heavy tractors and motor trucks, therefore freight traffic on the forestry railway drastically decreased. After most freight working had ended in the early 1970s a large part of the network was closed. Only the main line to Nagyrinya and the Kaszó branch line remained open for scheduled passenger trains and occasional timber trains. In 1975 only the 8 km long section between Szenta and Kaszó was still in service. The main line east of the of Bojsza kitérő loading point was dismantled even though the loading point was still used.

Until the 1980s the Hungarian army had some barracks in Kaszó. After the army had left, the Kaszó state forestry organisation converted the barracks into a hotel and opened the forests around Kaszó to the public. Nowadays the passenger trains are only run for tourists but for years the official timetable has been absolutely unreliable. The trains only run when ordered at the reception of the Kaszó Hotel! In 1997 3000 Forints (approximately £10) had to be paid to let the train run from Kaszó to Szenta and back. By Hungarian standards this is not cheap so the forestry railway is not used very often, and it was therefore surprising that the Kaszó forestry fully renewed the track and rolling stock in 1996.

Rolling Stock

Only diesel engines have been used on the relatively young Kaszó - Szenta Forestry Railway. Traffic started with a small B26 engine but in the 1950s and 1960s three second hand class C50 came to Kaszó and the B26 was withdrawn. These C50 had inside frames and were numbered C401 - C403. In the 1970s C403 was dumped on a side track at Kaszó, where today it is still standing. Around 1990 C401 was also withdrawn and the few trains were hauled solely by C402. In the spring of 1996 C401 was restored in the workshop of the MÁV agricultural railway at Balatonfenyves. Here a large Kaszó Forestry Railway logo was painted on the front of the now bright green loco and today both C401 and C402 are being used.

For the passenger service which started in 1961 the ÁEV bought a two-axle passenger coach with open platforms from the MÁV. The carriage was built for the Nyíregyháza narrow gauge local

In March 1963 an unknown photographer took this picture of a draisine and C50 number M15 (later C402) at Szenta. The characters in the group are interesting, from their dress well to do, perhaps with a family likeness, maybe even Hungarian gentry?
Photo: collection of Imre Balogh.

Reghin 0-8-0T 'Karácsony with a passenger train in the forests near Kaszó on 16th May 1998. Photo: Chikán Gábor.

railway (NyVKV) in 1905 and ran there until it was transferred to Kaszó. In 1996 this too was restored and painted bright green. Also the ÁEV also reconstructed a freight wagon, turning it into an open summer coach for the tourists.

In 1997 the Kaszó forestry organisation bought a Reghin steam engine from the Toplița - Borsec mineral water railway in Romania. The locomotive was named Karácsony (Christmas), and entered service on 22nd December 1997. It is only used for special trains.

Company Name

1952 - 1991:	ÁEV
1991:	Kaszó Erdőgazdaság Rt

Name of the Line

1952:	Kaszói Állami Erdei Vasút

Locomotives of the Kaszó Forestry Railway

Number(s)	Manufacturer	Class	In Service	Remarks
S17-204	SzBG (3069/1951)	B26	1951-1965	
M14; C401	Éfm (../1956)	C50	1956-now	ex-GV 3782 (Balatonfenyves)
M16; C402	Éfm (../..)	C50	? -now	ex-ÁEV Dalmand M16
C403	Éfm (../1956)	C50	1969- ?	ex-GV 3783 (Dombóvár)
Karácsony	Reg (603/1984)	0-8-0T	1998-now	ex-ApeMin 764.406R (Borsec)

There was just enough dappled sunlight for a picture of C402 and coach B09 in the forest near Bojsza on 17th July 1995.
Photo: Paul Engelbert.

The picturesque station of Kaszó is situated in the forests just outside the small village.
Photo: Paul Engelbert.

The Mesztegnyő Forestry Railway

South of the Mesztegnyő railway station on the standard gauge railway from Lake Balaton to Kaposvár a small sawmill is operated. In 1939 a six kilometre 760 mm gauge forestry railway was built between this sawmill and Nagyhomok to improve the timber supply out of the woods east of Mesztegnyő. The line was built with rails of 7 kg per metre. From the beginning the forestry railway was steam operated, but after the railway was nationalised in 1947 horses replaced the locomotive.

In 1958 and 1959 the Mesztegnyő - Nagyhomok forestry railway was extended and since then the main line has ended in the middle of nowwhere at a station called Felsőkak, 8.8 km east of Mesztegnyő. There are two branch lines. The first one starts at Szunyogvár and runs due south for four kilometres - it was abandoned in 1992 but in 1997 the track was renewed. The second branch line diverges near Mélyéger and also runs south, terminating in the forest after 1.2 km. The maximum speed on all lines is 15 km/h.

After the network had been extended traffic increased and locomotives were reintroduced to haul the little trains, which daily carried between 80 and 100 cubic metres of timber to the Mesztegnyő sawmill. Since 1959 passenger trains have run on the main line of the forestry railway between Mesztegnyő and Felsőkak. Remarkably they only ever ran on Tuesdays and Fridays and have been restricted to Fridays since 1997 but can also be hired on other days. The passengers are exclusively tourists visiting the forests and fish-filled lakes east of Mesztegnyő. Nowadays these trains are the only source of income for the railway.

The line is no longer being used on a regular basis by the forestry concern for the transport of timber as forest roads have made the railway superfluous since the 1980s. At the Mesztegnyő sawmill, however, railway trucks are still being used to transport the timber from the storage depot to the sawmill. Sometimes a loco shunts the trucks but most of the time the workmen push them by hand. Although the forestry railway does not flourish, the main line was fully renewed in 1995 and the old lightweight track was replaced using heavier 14.8 kg/m rails.

Rolling Stock

On the original Mesztegnyő - Nagyhomok forestry railway a small steam locomotive was used, bought second hand from the Kéthely brickyard. In 1947 the loco was diverted to the Süttő forestry railway.

Two small B26 class diesels came to Mesztegnyő in 1958, at least

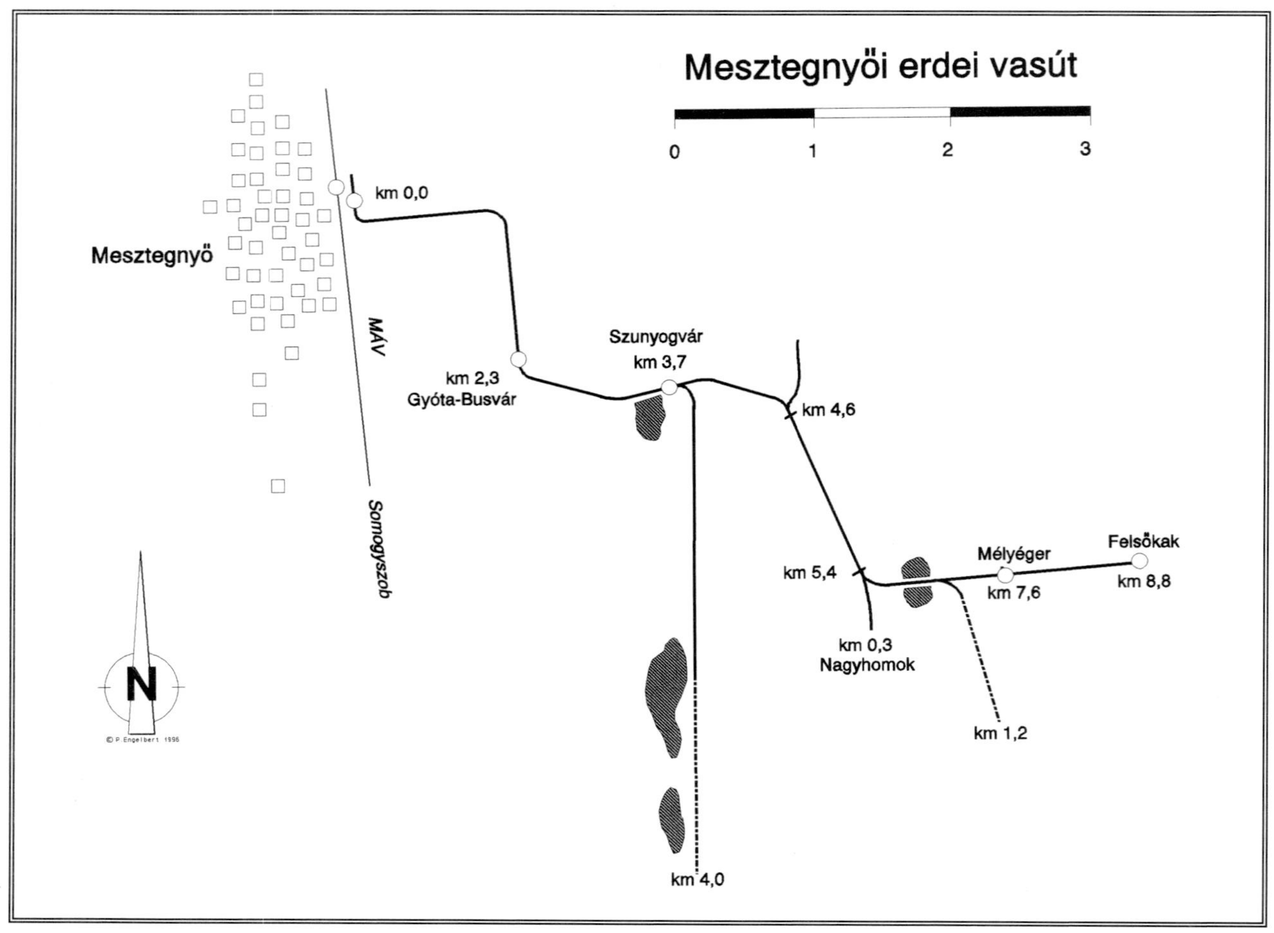

Small four wheel wagons are used to transport the timber within the premises of Mesztegnyő sawmill.
Photo: Paul Engelbert.

D22 with a short freight train at Mesztegnyő on 2nd April 1989.
Photo: Jörg Körner.

one of them having been taken over from the Vöröshalma - Bőszénfa forestry railway. In the 1960s two examples of the more powerful C50 were acquired from the Csepel iron works, replacing the class B26, and finally in 1983 two more C50s came to Mesztegnyő. Nowadays only class C50 numbers D22 and E04-047 are in working order, the latter of which was restored at Balatonfenyves in 1997/1998. The others were either dumped at Mesztegnyő or diverted elsewhere.

Two carriages are available for the passenger service. One is a two-axle carriage with an open platform, probably built for this line, and the other a four-axle Dunakeszi type that came in 1987 from the Gemenc forestry railway.

Company Name

1939 - 1947:	Berecz company
1947 - 1949:	MÁLLERD
1949 - 1991:	ÁEV
1991:	Somogyi Erdő- és Fafeldolgozó Gazdaság Rt

Name of the Line

1939 - 1949:	Mesztegnyő Erdei Vasút
1949:	Mesztegnyő Állami Erdei Vasút

Locomotives of the Mesztegnyő Forestry Railway

Number(s)	Manufacturer	Class	In Service	Remarks
?	KrMü (6148/1909)	0-6-0T (4bt)	1939-1947	ex-Kéthely brickyard; to Süttő
?	SzBG (../..)	B26	1958- ?	ex-ÁEV Bőszénfa
?	SzBG (../..)	B26	1958- ?	
C21	Éfm (../..)	C50	? - ?	from Csepel works
D22	Éfm (../..)	C50	? -now	from Csepel works
M1; E04-047	Éfm (../..)	C50	1983-now	
M2; E04-048	Éfm (../..)	C50	1983-now	

In the autumn of 1997 E04-047 was transported to Balatonfenyves. There she was restored by the workshop of the Balaton-fenyves economy railway. This photo depicts the loco about to be unloaded after arrival.
Photo: Imre Balogh.

On 20th December 1997 E04-047 looked as good as new again when photographed inside the Balaton-fenyves engine shed.
Photo: Imre Balogh.

The Almamellék Forestry Railway

Between 1901 and 1903 a short forestry railway was built which opened up the wide valleys in the Zselic region, south of Kaposvár. The main line ran from the MÁV station of Almamellék, half way along the Kaposvár - Szigetvár standard gauge line, to the sawmill at Sasrét. Another line started near the station of Almamellék and opened up the Terecseny valley. Both lines had short branches.

The network reached a length of 14 km, made up of track constructed with rails of 7, 9 and 10 kg/m, laid to a gauge of 600 mm. The maximum speed was initially fixed at 12 km/h but this was later reduced to only 8 km/h.

At first the railway was only used for the transportation of timber from the forests and the Sasrét sawmill to the MÁV railway station, but in 1960 the ÁEV started to run passenger trains on the Almamellék - Sasrét main line and on the Lukafa branch line.

In 1977 the MÁV closed the standard gauge railway from Kaposvár via Almamellék to Szigetvár, so it was no longer possible to transport the timber by rail from Almamellék to the customers who were situated all over the country. Even though in 1976 the narrow gauge trains were still carrying 30,000 cubic metres of timber to the railway station at Almamellék, timber transport on the forestry railway was almost completely diverted to road haulage.

Fortunately the passenger trains remained in service otherwise the network would probably no longer exist. Nevertheless a large part of the network was closed and only the Almamellék - Sasrét main line and the Lukafa branch line remained open. Only these lines were used for passenger trains and, because the lines were still in existence, they also saw the occasional timber train. Since 1989 the few remaining rail-hauled timber transports have been diverted to the road, however, the line was not officially closed for freight traffic. In 1997 a few occasional freight trains ran from Sasrét to Almamellék again and it may be that in future regular freight traffic will be resumed.

Meanwhile the situation of the passsenger traffic has become very precarious. According to the timetable the passenger train only runs once every weekday. Until 1996 there were officially two trains, but these hardly ever ran and if they did they were not on schedule. In 1997 the trains are reported to have run on schedule again but they did not always convey a passenger coach. The passengers, mainly forest workers, traveled on the small locomotive. Until recently groups of schoolchildren attending nature classes which were given at Sasrét, also travelled by train.

Rolling Stock

For many years the wagons were pulled by horses but since 1955 the ÁEV has used various types of lightweight locomotive on the railway. Apart from some diesel-engined class C50 there was also a 22 HP petrol-driven loco built by the Korány Emil works in Budapest. This is one of the few engines of the so called 'Hofherr' class to have run on a forestry railway in Hungary as normally these engines were used on industrial railways in mining districts.

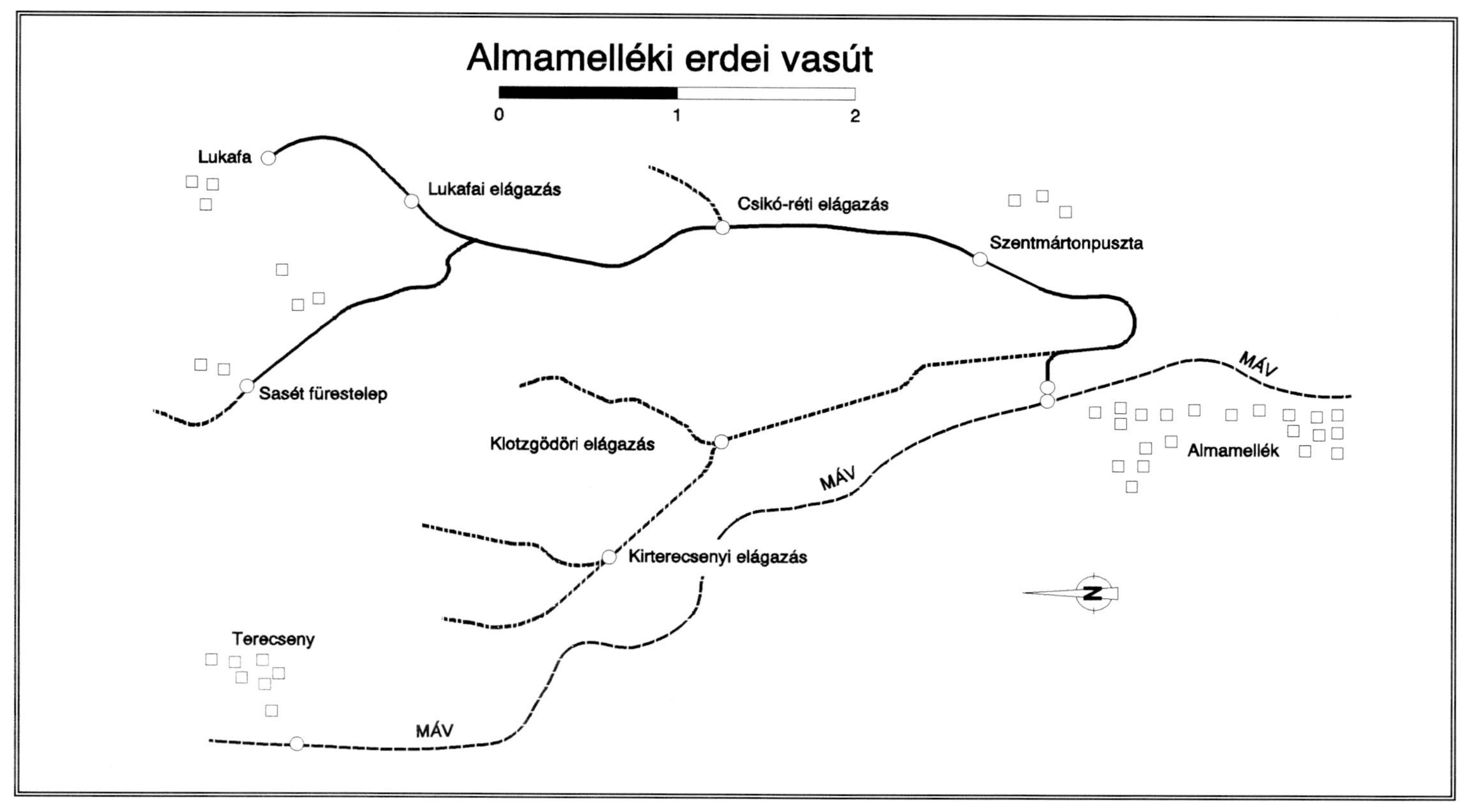

C22-403 with a train from Lukafá to Almamellék on 18th July 1995. The track on the left leads to Sasrét.
Photo: Paul Engelbert.

C22-403 hardly fits in the small engine shed at Almamellék.
Photo: Paul Engelbert.

Company Name

1901 - 1949:	Baron Biedermann
1949 - 1992:	ÁEV
1992:	Mecseki Erdészeti Rt

Name of the Line

1901 - 1949:	Almamelléki Erdei Vasút
1949:	Almamelléki Állami Erdei Vasút

For the passenger service the ÁEV used a two-axle passenger coach, which was in fact a reconstructed freight wagon. Nowadays there are two Dunakeszi class coaches, bought second-hand from the Királyrét Forestry Railway in 1970 and 1980.

Locomotives of the Almamellék Forestry Railway

Number(s)	Manufacturer	Class	In Service	Remarks
E21-201	KE (12355/1943)	Hofherr	1955-1964	ex-ÁEV Kemence
E21-204	PBJV (284-1/1954)	MD40	1965-1966	to ÁEV Vajszló
C21-403	Éfm (6203-921/1962)	C50	1962-now	
C21-404	Éfm (../..)	C50	1960s-1980s	
C21-406	KMD (6105-1769/1970)	C50	1969-1980	ex-GV 5704
C21-407	KMD (2126-8354/1970)	C50	1970-1987	ex-GV 5705
C22-403 (C21-408)	Éfm (6109-531/1963)	C50	1987-now	ex-ÁEV Vitézipuszta C22-403
E21-205	O&K (2138/1927)	MD2	1968-1970	

C22-403 at Lukafái elágazás station. Photo: Paul Engelbert.

Just before reaching the point where the line to Lukafa branches off C22-403 crosses a sandy road.
Photo: Paul Engelbert.

The Almamellék Forestry Railway passes through uninhabited forest and agricultural countryside.
Photo: Paul Engelbert.

The Gemenc Forestry Railway

The Gemenc forest is a well known nature reserve on the west bank of the River Danube near the town of Baja. Every year many thousands of tourists visit the 20,000 hectares of marshland, creeks and forests. A large part of the area is inaccesible to the public, but this does not prevent the forestry authorities from felling timber in the national park area.

In the 1950s four forestry railways existed in the Gemenc forests. The lines of Buvat, Fekete-erdő, Lassi and Gyűrűsalja connected cutting areas in the forests to timber storage points and the Danube shore. The first three railway lines, situated north of the MÁV standard gauge line, were later connected to or integrated into what is now the main line of the Gemenc Forestry Railway. The Gyűrűsalja Forestry Railway, situated south of the standard gauge line, remained isolated from the new forestry railway network.

The main line of the Gemenc Forestry Railway ran from Keselyüs via Gemenc to Pörböly, a distance of 24 kilometres. The Keselyüs - Gemenc section was probably already open by 1960 and the line from Gemenc to Pörböly was completed in 1963. The Szomfova branch followed six years later making a total length of more than 30 kilometres.

The track was built with rails of only 7 kg per metre but soon heavier rail of 18 kg/m was laid. The maximum speed was fixed at 30 km/h but reduced to 10 km/h in the 1980s, however, the condition of the permanent way is now excellent. The track has been rebuilt with heavy rail of 18, 23.6, and even 34.5 kg per metre, mounted on concrete sleepers.

In the good years narrow gauge trains transported some 30,000 cubic meters of timber to the Pörböly sawmill. Nowadays tractors and lorries are also used and the trains only carry about 7,500 cubic meters or 6,000 tons of timber annually. The branch lines, which were only seldom used after the freight volume had dropped, were closed by 1990 and by that time only the branches to Szomfova and Gemenc dunapart were still in existence. These remained in situ and the latter was reopened in 1995. Because Gemenc is a very swampy area it is almost impossible to use heavy lorries so timber is still being transported by rail. The trains run on most weekdays and regulary arrive at Pörböly early in the morning, however, shunting can be observed for a few hours after the train has arrived.

The railway is also used for passenger traffic. From 1963 a public passenger service was in operation between Gemenc and Keselyüs and in 1966 passenger trains also started running between Pörböly and Lovasfok. Even in the first season 10,000 tourists frequented the trains leaving Pörböly. Through passenger traffic between

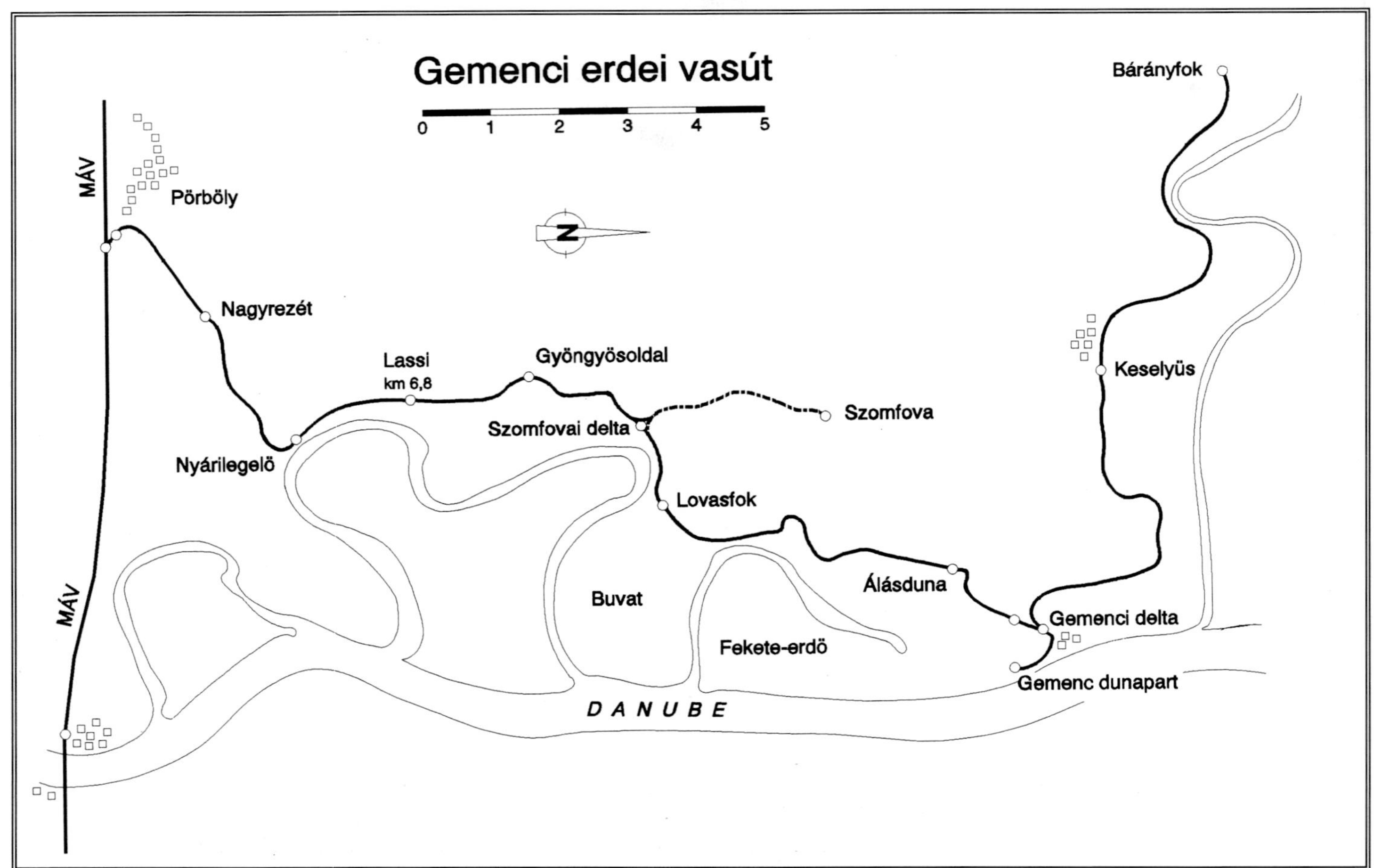

CDH24-405 stands beside the wooden shelter at Pörböly station, having just arrived.
Photo: Author's collection.

On 8th July 1996 CDH24-407 was shunting some timber on the typical little trucks at Pörböly sawmill.
Photo: Paul Engelbert.

Gemenc and Pörböly has never existed and the trains from Pörböly to Szomfova and from Gemenc to Szomfova are run separately.

In 1983 the main line was extended from Keselyüs to Bárányfok. The new 6 km long section was built for passenger trains only and proved to be a great succes. The number of passengers rose to 100,000 a year, but since the revolution of 1989 the railway has lost much of its popularity. In 1994 only 36,700 passengers were counted and by 1997 this number had dropped to 29,500.

Trains do not run according to schedule, particularly on weekdays. Only if there are passengers waiting will a train be sent up the line into the forests. The running of the train is adjusted to the schedule of the freight and maintenance trains and, perhaps most important, to the mood of the train personnel. For instance, trains which should run from Pörböly to Szomfova turn back at Lassi. It also happens that a passenger coach may be simply coupled to a freight train which is just about to leave Pörböly. Anyone who wants to take a trip on the Gemenc forestry railway should be warned about the many millions of mosquitos which live in the swampy forests. Even with anti-mosquito oil and long sleeves the one hour ride can be very unpleasant.

Rolling Stock

The original short forestry railways were horse worked, though shortly after they were connected diesel traction was also introduced. It is not known which locomotives were used before 1964 but in that year the first two class C50, C24-401 and C24-402, came to Gemenc and between 1966 and 1978 five more followed, C24-403 - C24-407. All these locomotives were bought second hand from the MÁV GV or came from other ÁEV lines after they had been closed, so they were not all painted in a uniform livery.

The new class Z90 locomotive, C50Z-404, at Pörböly on 20th September 1997.
Photo: Chikán Gábor.

In 1990 and 1991 the original diesel mechanical driving units of five remaining locomotives were replaced by diesel hydraulic units. Because the new engines are somewhat larger a lot of the pipework and the grill are mounted on the outside of the engine compartment. The locos were also painted in a dark green livery and renumbered from class C24 into class CDH24 (DH stands for diesel hydraulic).

In 1997 CDH24-404 was again reconstructed and renumbered to C50Z-404. This time an almost new diesel loco (type Z90) was created, hardly recognisable as a class C50. The 90kW diesel engine makes it more than twice as powerful as a regular class C50.

A wide range of coaches are available for the passenger service. Normally the summer coaches constructed by the railway itself are used, but there are also some Dunakeszi and former MÁV GV Bak coaches. For timber transport the railway uses both bogie platform wagons and two-axle bolster wagons.

Company Name

1963 - 1992:	ÁEV
1992:	Gemenci Erdő- és Vadgazdaság Rt

Name of the Line

1963:	Gemenci Állami Erdei Vasút

Locomotives of the Gemenc Forestry Railway

Number(s)	Manufacturer	Class	In Service	Remarks
C24-401	Éfm (../..)	C50	1964 - 1991	ex-GV 3787 (Sajószentpéter)
C24-402; C24-404'	Éfm (../..)	C50	1964 - 1991	ex-GV 3786 (Sajószentpéter)
C24-403	Éfm (../..)	C50	1966 - 1991	ex-GV 3751 (Mezőkovácsháza)
C24-404	Éfm (../1952)	C50	1966 - ?	ex-GV 4502 (Szerencs), (scrapped)
C24-405	Éfm (../..)	C50	1966 - 1990	ex-GV 3791 (Szob)
C24-406	Éfm (../1952)	C50	1968 - 1977	ex-Dalmand M1; ex-GV 3706
C24-407	Éfm (../1955)	C50	1978 - 1991	ex-GV 3767 (Balatonfenyves)
CDH24-401	BaMü (../1991)	CDH50	1991 - now	formerly C24-401
CDH24-403	BaMü (../1991)	CDH50	1991 - now	formerly C24-403
CDH24-404	BaMü (../1991)	CDH50	1991 - 1996	formerly C24-404' (formerly C24-402)
CDH24-405	BaMü (../1990)	CDH50	1990 - now	formerly C24-405
CDH24-407	BaMü (../1991)	CDH50	1991 - now	formerly C24-407
C50Z-404	FKG (../1997)	Z90 (C50Z)	1997 - now	formerly CDH24-404

CDH24-407 with a maintenance train in the forests near Nyárilegelő on 11th July 1996.

Photo: Paul Engelbert.

Logs are transported on heavy four-axle flat wagons such as this one and on small two-axle trucks.

Photo: Paul Engelbert.

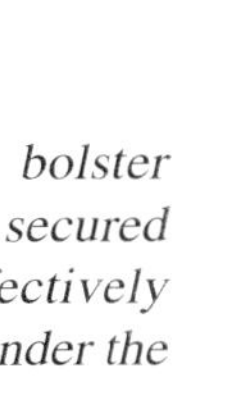

Examples of the four wheel bolster wagons, showing the timber secured between the stanchions, effectively using the little trucks as bogies under the load.

Photo: Paul Engelbert.

Known Forestry Railways

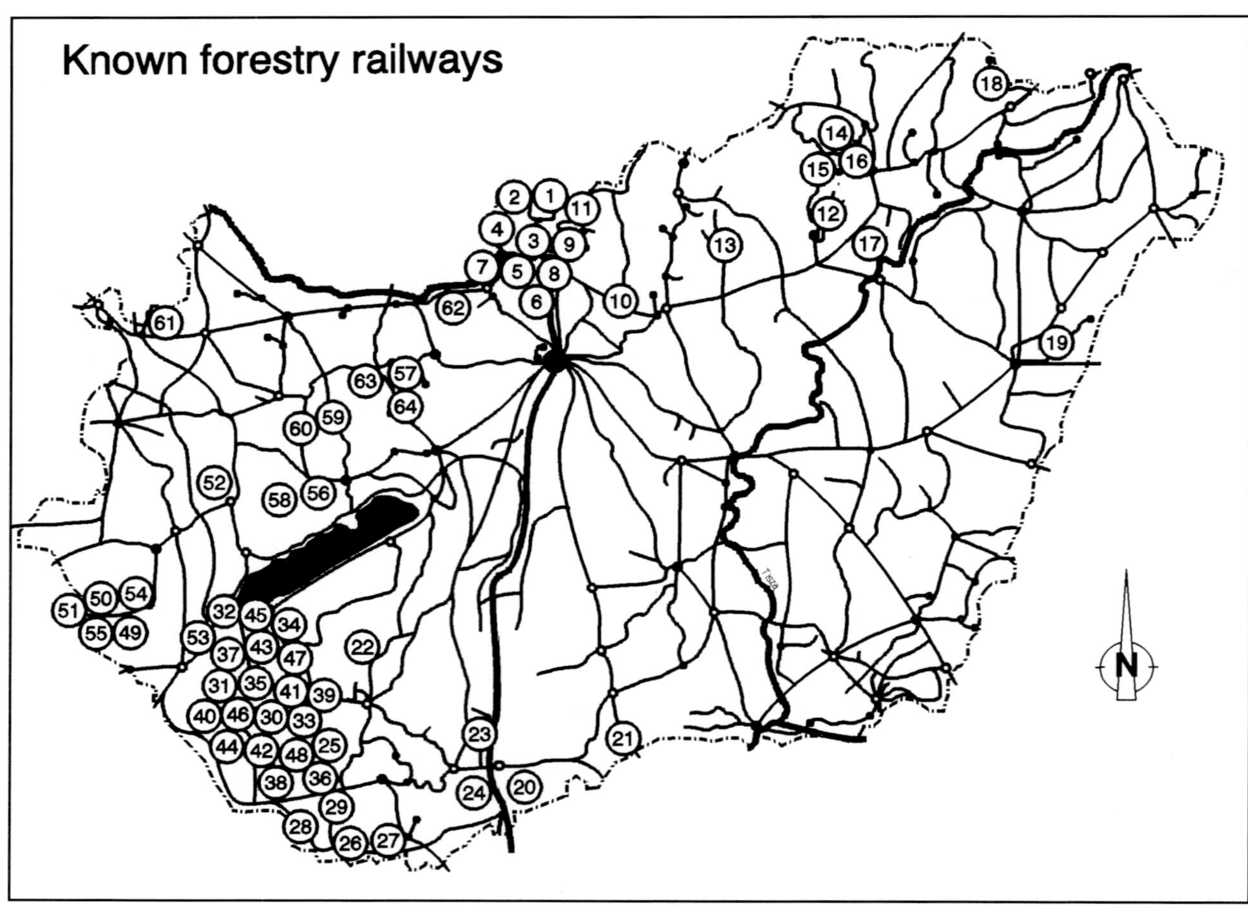

In this list the approximate length, the original gauge and the operational period of the known permanent forestry railways are summarised. This list does not pretend to be complete but only shows those lines whose existence could be confirmed. Undoubtedly many more forestry railways than those listed below existed in Hungary. Forestry railways which later merged into another forestry railway network are not mentioned. Known lines, whether still open or already closed, are geographically arranged by district. Lines with passenger traffic are marked P.

Line		Length	Gauge	Opened	Closed	Remarks
Pest district						
1	Bernecebaráti	7 km	600 mm	..	..	
2	Kemence	51 km	600 mm	1915	1992	track remains
3	Királyrét (old)	23 km	600 mm	1893	1979	P
3	Királyrét (new)	11 km	760 mm	1981	-	P; pioneer forestry railway
4	Nagybörzsöny (old)	29 km	600 mm	1908	1920	
4	Nagybörzsöny (new)	55 km	760 mm	1920	1992	P; no traffic 1980-89; museum
5	Dömös	6 km	..	..	..	
6	Lepence	2 km	..	..	..	
7	Pilismarót	6 km	..	..	..	
8	Visegrád	7 km	760 mm	1921	1932	
Nógrád district						
9	Diósjenő	6 km	600 mm	1947	..	
10	Galgamácsa	6 km	760 mm	1920s	1963	
11	Nagyoroszi	16 km	600 mm	..	..	

Heves district						
12	Felsőtárkány	30 km	760 mm	1915	-	P
13	Gyöngyös	46 km	600 mm	1906	-	P; 1922 regauged to 760 mm
14	Nagyvisnyó	15 km	600 mm	..	1968	
15	Szilvásvárad	22 km	600 mm	1908	-	P; 1948 regauged to 760 mm
Borsod-Abaúj-Zemplén district						
16	Lillafüred	45 km	760 mm	1920	-	P
17	Nagymihály	..	760 mm	..	..	
18	Pálháza	14 km	700 mm	1888	-	P; 1947 regauged to 760 mm
Hajdú-Bihar district						
19	Debrecen	36 km	950 mm	1882	(1922)	P; converted into economy rly
Bács-Kiskun district						
20	Pandúr (Szeremle)	15 km	760 mm	1926	1970s	
21	Kelebia	12 km	760 mm	..	1950s	
Tolna district						
22	Dalmand	5 km	760 mm	..	1978	P
23	Gemenc (Pörböly)	35 km	760 mm	1960	-	P
24	Gyűrűsalja (Béda)	17 km	760 mm	1930	1970s	
Baranya district						
25	Almamellék	13 km	600 mm	1901	-	P
26	Csányoszró	5 km	600 mm	1946	1978	
27	Vajszló	7 km	760 mm	1924	1971	1952 regauged to 600 mm
28	Vitézipuszta	21 km	600 mm	1922	1983	
29	Szentegát (Szigetvár)	9 km	600 mm	..	(1949)	line taken over by GVI
Somogy district						
30	Alsóbogát (Beleg)	6 km	600 mm	..	..	
31	Alsósegesd	3 km	600 mm	..	..	
32	Balatonszentgyörgy	7 km	760 mm	..	..	
33	Bőszénfa	5 km	760 mm	..	1957	
34	Buzsák	6 km	600 mm	..	..	
35	Dávod	7 km	600 mm	..	..	
36	Gyöngyöspuszta (Lad)	6 km	600 mm	..	..	
37	Gyótapuszta	6 km	600 mm	..	..	
38	Homokszentgyörgy	5 km	600 mm	..	..	
39	Kaposvár (Ropoly)	23 km	600 mm	..	..	
40	Kaszó	30 km	760 mm	1952	-	P
41	Kiskorpád	11 km	600 mm	..	..	
42	Lábod	4 km	600 mm	..	..	
43	Mesztegnyő	15 km	760 mm	1939	-	P
44	Simongát (old)	9 km	600 mm	1899	1948	
44	Simongát (new)	7 km	760 mm	1970	1979	P
45	Somogyszentpál	3 km	760 mm	..	..	
46	Somogyszob	5 km	760 mm	1920s	1950s	
47	Somogyvár (Vidámház)	7 km	600 mm	..	..	
48	Titványpuszta (Lad)	7 km	600 mm	..	..	
Zala district						
49	Csömödér	75 km	760 mm	1918	-	P
50	Lenti	35 km	760 mm	1923	-	

51	Rédics	39 km	760 mm	1914	1924	
52	Zalaerdőd	..	..	..	..	
53	Zalakomár (Pát)	24 km	760 mm	..	..	track at Pát fish farm still used
54	Ortaháza	12 km	..	..	..	
55	Vétyempuszta	8 km	760 mm	..	1948	connected to Csömöder
Veszprém district						
56	Úrkút	9 km	600 mm	1883	1953	
57	Császár	..	..	..	..	
58	Devecser	..	..	..	..	
59	Vinye	15 km	760 mm	..	1958	track at Vinye sawmill still used
60	Franciavágás (Városlőd)	46 km	760 mm	1910	1976	P; regauged to 600 mm
Győr-Sopron district						
61	Eszterháza	58 km	760 mm	1947	(1949)	line taken over by GVI
Komárom-Esztergom district						
62	Süttő	17 km	760 mm	..	1973	P
63	Réde	..	760 mm	..	..	
Fejér district						
64	Bodajk	..	..	..	..	

Empty stock being pushed from Törosnek to Pördefolde on the Csömödér system. Loading took place with the wagons standing on the main line at Pördefolde. Photo: Paul Engelbert 20th July 1995.

Abbreviations

ÁEV	Állami Erdei Vasutak (State Forestry Railways)
ApeMin	Ape Minerale, Borsec (Romania)
BaMü	MÁV Bajai Műhely
BkGV	Bodrogkőzi Gazdasági Vasút (Bodrog region economy railway)
Bp	Budapest Works, Budapest; after 1945 MÁVAG
CGV	Ceglédkörnyéki Gazdasági Vasút (Cegléd region economy railway)
DHF	Deutsche Heeresfeldbahn (German military railways)
Éfm	MÁV Északi Főműhelye, Budapest (Északi Fm)
FÁEV	Felsőtárkányi Állami Erdei Vasút
FGV	Fekete Garamvölgyi Vasút (ČHŽ Čiernohronská Forest Railway, Hronec, Slovakia)
FKG	Felépitménykarbantartó Gépgyár, Jászkisér
Flor	Lokomotivfabrik Floridsdorf
GEV	Görgényivölgyi Erdei Vasút (Gurghiu Forestry Railway; Hungary/Romania)
GV	Gazdasági Vasút (economy railway)
GVI	Gazdasági Vasutak Igazgatosága (direction for economy railways)
Jung	Arnold Jung Lokomotivfabrik GmbH, Jungenthal, Germany
KE	Korány Emil, Budapest
KGV	Kecskeméti Gazdasági Vasút (Kecskemét economy railway)
kkHB	kaiserlich-königliche Heeresbahn (Austro-Hungarian military railways)
KMD	MÁV Kisvasutak Műhely, Dombovár (MÁV narrow gauge workshop)
KrMü	Lokomotivfabrik Krauss & Comp, München, Germany
LÁEV	Lillafüredi Állami Erdei Vasút (Lillafüred state forestry rly)
MÁEV	Mátrai Állami Erdei Vasút, Gyöngyös
Maf	J.A. Maffei AG, München, Germany
MÁLLERD	Magyar Állami Erdőgazdasági Üzemek (Hungarian State Forestry Company)
MÁV	Magyar Államvasutak (Hungarian state railways)
MÁVAG	Magyar Állami Vas-, Ácél- és Gépgyárak, Budapest, Hungary
M&F	F. Marinelli & L. Faccanoni, Wien (Vienna)
NyVKV	Nyíregyháza Vidéki Kisvasút (Nyíregyháza region narrow gauge railway)
O&K	Orenstein & Koppel AG, Budapest or Berlin
PBJV	Pálfalvai Bányagépgyártó és Javító Vállalát, Zagyva-pálfalva
Reg	Reghin, Romania
Reş	Reşiţa, Romania
Rt	Részvénytársaság (company)
WrN	AG der Lokomotivfabrik vorm. G. Sigl Lokomotivfabrik Wiener Neustadt, Austria
ZB	Zillertalbahn, Jenbach, Austria

Bibliography

In addition to the research in primary sources during many visits to Hungary the following secondary sources were consulted:

Endre Bajcsy: Gyöngyös Mátravasút, Tájak-Korok-Múzeumok Kiskönyvtára 529, TKM, Budapest, 1996.
Imre Balogh: Kisvasút a Nagyberekben, Balatonfenyves, 1996.
Roland Beier, Hans Hufnagel: Wälder und Dampf (Vol II), Hufnagel/Beier, Wien, 1993.
Karel Beneš: Vasúti Közlekedés Kárpátalján, MÁV Rt, Budapest, 1996.
József Csiba, Alfréd Falk: A MÁV Gépgyár és a MÁVAG gőzmozdony szállításai külföldre; in: Vasúthistória évkönyv 1990, MÁV Rt. Vezérigazgatósága, Budapest, 1990.
Keith Chester: East European Narrow Gauge, Locomotives International, Clevedon, 1994.
Hans Herbert Frohn: Schmalspurbahnen in Ungarn, in: Die Kleinbahn 28, Verlag Zeunert, Gifhorn, 1967.
Miklós Herczeg, Sándor Malatinszky: Az úttörővasúttól a gyermekvasútig, MÁV Rt. Vezérigazgatósága, Budapest, 1996.
Erzsébet Juhász: A Székely körvasút és a kapcsolódó vasúthálozat története (1866-1944); in: Vasúthistória évkönyv 1990, MÁV Rt. Vezérigazgatósága, Budapest, 1990.
Zolt Károly: Die Királyreter Waldbahn, in: Eisenbahn 12/1974, Bohmnann Verlag, Wien.
Mihály Kubinszky: Dampf in der Puszta, Verlag Slezak, Wien, 1978.
Zoltán Szűcs, Gábor Chikán: A Kárpát-Medence Kisvasútjainak Járművei (Lista), Budapest, 1997.
Zoltán Thorday: Kisvasutak Magyarországon, MÁV vezérigazgatóság, Budapest, 1989.

Periodicals:
Eisenbahn Österreich, Bohmann Verlag, Wien / MINIREX AG, Luzern
LOK Report, AG LOK Report, Münster
KBK Füzetek, Kisvasutak baráti köre, Budapest
Hivatalos Menetrend, (Hungarian timetable), MÁV, Budapest
Informationen-760, Club 760, Murau

Internet sites:
http:\\www.ttt.bme.hu\kbk\kbk.html

D02-508 on the bridge over the deep Mélyvölgy valley west of Papírgyár.
Photo: Chikán Gábor, 13th May 1995.